The Jossey-Bass
Nonprofit & Public Management Series
also includes:

Forging Nonprofit Alliances

The National Alliance for Nonprofit Management (Alliance) is the result of the 1998 merger of The Support Centers of America and the Nonprofit Management Association. The purpose of the Alliance is to challenge and strengthen those who deliver management support to nonprofit organizations. Members include management support organizations, individual professionals, and a range of national and regional, umbrella, academic, publishing, and philanthropic organizations that provide technical assistance (training and consulting) to nonprofits. By raising the bar on quality among its members and its member's clients, the Alliance provides leadership in the enhancement of a broader vision . . . one of health communities and a stronger civil society.

Contact information:
The National Alliance for Nonprofit Management
1899 L Street, NW
3rd floor
Washington, D.C. 20036
E-mail: NANMlp@aol.com

Forging Nonprofit Alliances

A Comprehensive Guide
to Enhancing Your
Mission Through

- Joint Ventures and Partnerships
- Management Service Organizations
- Parent Corporations
- Mergers

Jane Arsenault

A publication of
The National Alliance for Nonprofit Management

Jossey-Bass Publishers • San Francisco

Jossey-Bass books and products are available through most bookstores. To contact
Jossey-Bass directly, call (888) 378-2537, fax to (800) 605-2665, or visit our website
at www.josseybass.com.

Substantial discounts on bulk quantities of Jossey-Bass books are available to
corporations, professional associations, and other organizations. For details and
discount information, contact the special sales department at Jossey-Bass.

For sales outside the United States, please contact your local Simon & Schuster
International Office.

Library of Congress Cataloging-in-Publication Data

Arsenault, Jane.
    Forging nonprofit alliances: a comprehensive guide to enhancing your mission
through joint ventures and partnerships, management service organizations,
parent corporations, mergers/Jane Arsenault.—1st ed.
      p. cm.—(The Jossey-Bass nonprofit & public management series)
    "A publication of the National Alliance for Nonprofit Management."
    Includes bibliographical references (p.   ) and index.
    ISBN 0-7879-1003-1 (alk. paper)
    1. Nonprofit organizations. 2. Consolidation and merger of corporations.
3. Strategic alliances (Business) I. National Alliance for Nonprofit Management.
II. Title. III. Title: Forging non-profit alliances. IV. Series: Jossey-Bass nonprofit
and public management series.
HD2769.15.A77   1998
658'.044—dc21   98–7508

FIRST EDITION
HB Printing 10 9 8 7 6 5 4 3 2 1

The Jossey-Bass
Nonprofit & Public Management Series

To my family: Raymond, Gregory, Anne, and Michael.
Each, by patience, encouragement, hands-on help,
or simple willingness to do without me for a while longer,
has contributed to my ability to complete this work.

Contents

Resources

Preface

As many nonprofits have discovered to their cost, an organization's own structure—its corporate identity—can impede its ability to compete for the resources necessary for survival. In my consulting practice, I have spent a majority of my time in the last three years helping organizations explore changes in corporate structure as a tool to protect and enhance their mission and to manage in the face of major environmental challenges. In each instance, my clients and I have had to work through the basic concepts together, as there were few written sources to support the process of making these decisions. This book aims to fill that gap, capturing the decision process needed to support the restructuring effort in terms that reflect the perspective of nonprofit management.

The options defined in these pages—joint ventures and partnerships, management service organizations, parent corporations, and mergers—can be powerful tools to enhance mission accomplishment. This book is designed to provide supports to the process of determining whether these options are appropriate for a particular organization's purpose, to describe the process of negotiating the agreements on which alliances are based, and to provide insight into the challenges of making the transition to the new entity.

As I speak at conferences and work with clients, I hear from executive directors who are facing the challenge of integrating what their organizations do into a more cohesive system. They tell me that the pressure is increasing to integrate across disciplines in one field of service after another. The lack of naturally existing relationships between or among CEOs can be a particular challenge in building networks that are *horizontal* (involving continuums of service) and in building networks that are *cross-disciplinary* (such as job-related services with mental health and domestic violence). These

CEOs face the challenge of negotiating with partners where there is neither knowledge nor trust. They are often perplexed about how to structure the new relationships, worrying most about balancing local control against the centralization of control for the joint effort or system.

Other arenas in which these same concerns arise are regional conferences of organizations that are similar or that are linked by a shared national office. These groups are increasingly exploring ways to work more effectively together. I also find these questions raised among small groups of organizations from the same field, who may have been meeting for years to share common problems and approaches. They, too, sense that their informal network might be made more valuable but lack the knowledge to make it so. These groups have an advantage in that the CEOs are often colleagues and friends and are well known to one another, lending a base of trust and support. Some also say that this familiarity is a weakness, incorporating as it does what may be long-standing enmities, jealousies, and personality conflicts that somehow must be managed in a new structure.

In my nonprofit community of southern New England, I have watched several organizations make costly errors in judgment because their leadership was not fully informed of the alternatives available to them. I have seen organizations attempt mergers and fail, when some less onerous form of alliance might have served equally well—and I have seen loose and free-form relationships fall apart when a more centralized model would have accomplished the intended purpose.

I am personally motivated by a profound concern for the future of the sector and worry that the significant changes in management expectations will result in the loss of community control over services. As I see it, the task of managing a nonprofit is becoming so complex that small, locally based organizations will not be able to compete for resources or consumers. When I discuss this with colleagues, there is real pain in their expressions of concern that only mega-agencies may remain. I believe that some of the models discussed in this book may help protect the concept and practice of local governance.

In addition, my practice has brought me in contact with a large number of health care agencies who, due to the incursion of managed care, have been forced—often precipitously—to consider corporate restructuring. The models they have chosen to accomplish this forced consolidation come mostly from the for-profit sector—and, in some cases, these models have been adopted without alteration. But I have also noticed that some groups of organizations are adapting the adaptations and are creating new kinds of organizations that capture both the value of the for-profit model and the *value system* of nonprofits, creating new variations that are uniquely suited to the sector. It is my belief that these variations may benefit a wide array of organizational types: cultural, artistic, and environmental, as well as health and human services. This is the good news I hope to share.

Audience

Executive directors and Board members interested in examining their options will find this book particularly useful. It may also be helpful to consultants and legal counsel who count nonprofit organizations among their clients. The material included here is not to be considered as a substitute for legal counsel or for consulting support, but should enable Board members and executive staff to have informed discussions with these professional advisers.

It is also my hope that this material will attract an audience beyond health and human service agencies. As noted earlier, some of the innovations described here have the potential to solve thorny problems that have beset the sector for a long time, such as the lack of management infrastructure in fields dominated by a large number of small nonprofits, such as arts, preservation, environmental, and other kinds of advocacy. I have tried to include a variety of examples and applications so as to help a wide range of nonprofit leadership see themselves and their organizations in the material.

I will be very pleased, as well, if the staff of foundations and state funding sources also find the book helpful, expanding their knowledge of what it takes to restructure a nonprofit. Perhaps this material will also help them build empathy for grantees facing the challenges of these processes.

To address concerns about language, wherever possible, I have couched the discussion in words that nonprofit leaders will feel comfortable with while simultaneously offering the more commonly used business terms for these discussions. In the end, I believe that including both sets of vocabulary will make it easier to discuss this material with our Board members who come to us from the business community. Should any of these Board members be readers, it may also help them apply what they already know about corporate restructuring to the circumstances of the nonprofits they serve.

Structure

Chapter One explores how your organization can discover potential opportunities for consolidation. Chapter Two looks at how your organization can prepare for negotiations that you will initiate and for responding when your organization has been approached by another to participate in a new venture. Chapters Three through Six explore each of the four models currently available for nonprofits considering restructuring: joint ventures and partnerships, management service organizations, parent corporations, and mergers.

The remaining chapters apply to all four options. Chapter Seven discusses early stage negotiations, while Chapter Eight describes formal negotiations, including the use of professional advisers. Chapter Nine deals with issues involved in designing both the governance structure and operations of the new entity. Chapter Ten discusses integration of corporate cultures, and Chapter Eleven defines the process for ratifying final agreements, communicating with external constituents, and designing the transition plan.

Nothing (Jointly) Ventured. . . .

I have been told again and again by colleagues who are in positions of nonprofit leadership that this is "tough stuff." Yes, it is. Why is it so hard?

First of all, many of us within the sector don't like to think of the entities we manage as corporations. We prefer *organization* or *agency* or *community group* or *association*. Some of us are actively repelled by the language of the corporate world. Unfortunately, most of what has been written about these processes is written in the language of business, and while some of us are getting used to the idea that we are managing social-purpose businesses, many of us still resist thinking of our nonprofit as a business enterprise. As well, discussion of restructuring involves dealing with our legal identity and requires mastery of some legal terms.

Another concern raised by colleagues is the complexity of the process of consolidation. As my own knowledge of what it takes to build a successful consolidation has increased through my consulting practice and through additional research, I have become convinced that the complexity is, for the most part, necessary. I have also discovered, though, that these processes stretch themselves out over a substantial amount of time—six to twelve months of negotiation and another twelve to eighteen months to complete the transition. The tasks outlined here are not the work of one horrible two-week retreat; they can be dealt with comfortably over the two to three years that the process involves.

Nonetheless, the complexity can seem intimidating up front, and there are weightier reasons for a reluctance to contemplate restructuring. Some of us hesitate to look at these options because we know that nonprofit governing Boards are in charge of corporate identity. Changing this part of the organization requires intense engagement of Board members—and some already feel frustration at the lack of engagement of our Boards and will hesitate to involve them in such complex decision making. In any case, there are no readily available models for this involvement.

These decisions are legally binding and involve alteration in the ability of our organization to engage in fully autonomous decision making. All the options require us to share power to some extent. Some of them involve significant changes in the positions of staff, managers, executive leadership, and Board members, changes that may range from additional responsibilities to redesigned jobs to eliminated positions—and that is potentially painful. There aren't very many of us who seek out potentially painful situations on purpose.

One of the very helpful reviewers who ably critiqued an earlier version of my manuscript put it this way, "Why, why, why? Why think about this now? Why involve our Board in such dramatic change, when we are trying to get them more active in our current needs? Why operate in such a different manner?"

From my perspective, there is only one answer to that question that is worth stating. It is worth our time to add these tools to our strategic options because they offer so much to our ability to accomplish our missions in a turbulent world. It is my hope that this book will assist nonprofit leadership not only to learn how to think this way but to learn how to recognize *when* it is important to think this way and to be able to identify the full range of options available. Only then will intelligent, informed, and fully effective decisions be reached as to which of these tools should be used, when, and by whom.

Acknowledgments

First, I thank all my clients who have struggled with the hard choices of consolidating their organizations, and who have allowed me to share their experiences. From them, I learned what I needed to know to help others. In particular, I want to acknowledge the encouragement of the Collaboration Committee of Kent County Mental Health Center (KCMHC) and Westbay Community Action, who willingly served as guinea pigs for some early draft materials, and the support of David S. Lauterbach, CEO of KCMHC, who always assured me that I have something worthwhile to teach. I also want to thank members of the Joint Planning Committee of Child and Family Services of Newport County and Riverwood Mental Health Services, who asked me to develop the initial version of the tool to allocate power within a parent corporation model.

And I thank Rick Smith, former executive director of The Support Centers of America, who has provided encouragement and good counsel, patiently, throughout the project.

May 1998   JANE ARSENAULT
Lincoln, Rhode Island

The Author

JANE ARSENAULT has served as a management consultant for nonprofit organizations and organizations that fund nonprofits for the last eighteen years. She has concentrated her practice in five key areas: strategic planning and market analysis, program evaluation, governance, conflict management, and most recently, consolidation models. In addition to consulting with nonprofits, she has spent approximately two hundred hours annually in a variety of teaching and training settings. Her work brings her into contact with the management of organizations throughout the many fields of the nonprofit sector, including health, human services, libraries, arts organizations, and environmental groups.

She began her work with the nonprofit community as executive director of the Rhode Island office of Opportunities for Women in 1977. Her interest in evaluation and in management assistance grew from her work as manager of training, technical assistance, and evaluation for the United Way of Southeastern New England, a position she held from 1980 through 1986. During the last twelve years, she has consulted with over three hundred nonprofit organizations in southern New England, serving as executive director of The Support Center of Rhode Island from 1993 to 1997.

In addition to client work, she is involved in a number of other projects. One is the composition of the answers to the most frequently asked questions about program evaluation to be published on the Internet as part of the Clearinghouse on NonProfit Management, a project of The Support Centers of America. Another current effort is the facilitation of two learning communities based in Rhode Island. One deals with the concept of consumers as partners in the design and delivery of human services. The other is exploring the question of the effectiveness of traditional governance models in the current turbulent climate for nonprofits.

She is a graduate of Hunter College of the City of New York, where she earned a Bachelor's Degree *cum laude* with Departmental Honors in English Literature. She received her Master's Degree in Business Administration from the Executive MBA Program of the University of Rhode Island.

Forging Nonprofit Alliances

Part One

When Mission Matters Most

Chapter One

Discovering Strategic Opportunities

Looking across the fields that make up the nonprofit sector, three basic scenarios seem to inspire organizations to consider some form of consolidation:

1. *Survival as an autonomous unit is in doubt, and an organization's leadership desires to ensure survival of all or part of its activities.* An organization's leaders may become convinced that solo survival is unlikely when they assess the changes likely to occur in the environment or the organization's relative strength in comparison to current or emerging competition. Sudden events such as loss of a sustaining government contract may force these conclusions precipitously. While some might view this conviction as equivalent to acceptance of failure, it is not necessarily that at all. If people believe that the organization has something worth saving, something that will still contribute toward mission accomplishment, they can pursue consolidation wholeheartedly—and any productive survival is a form of success.

2. *The organization's leadership sees an opportunity to build dominance or leadership in a particular service arena (or market).* On the other hand, an organization's leaders may recognize that they have such substantial resources that they can afford to use them to take strategic advantage of environmental change. Such an organization can expand its reach and impact through partnership with or acquisition of smaller or less well-positioned organizations, or it can share its resources with other similarly strong organizations to multiply its impact.

3.   *The organization needs additional resources to pursue an opportunity or maintain or increase a commitment to mission-driven programming.* This third scenario occurs when an organization's leaders recognize that they have a program or resource that could contribute to mission if sufficiently strengthened by added competencies, facilities, financial resources, or management expertise. To maximize the effort's potential, leadership seeks a partner to fill in the resource gap.

This scenario also applies to building *continuums,* when organizations link together sequential services, each organization contributing one or more of the programmatic elements.

Deciding to Decide

There is some debate about how nonprofit leaders come to the conclusion that one of these scenarios fits their organization. To date, no well-articulated process has emerged, and some view these occurrences as happenstance, an opportunity stumbled upon, or necessity, something that can't be avoided. It is true that recognition does occur in these ways. It is also true, however, that recognition often comes to one or two people, who then face the challenge of convincing the rest that this is the right thing to do.

In my consulting practice, the recognition occurs increasingly as the result of strategic planning processes that are comprehensive and inclusive. The balanced participation of Board and staff in strategic planning creates a context for these significant decisions. Does that mean that strategic planning is the only path and that your organization has to undertake an entire strategic planning process to figure this out? No—but for those who are not faced with making immediate decisions and who have the opportunity (time) to engage in thoughtful consideration of these issues, it is helpful to frame these considerations in a broader inquiry that defines all of an organization's options. A recent publication of the Boston Foundation, *The Rush to Merge,* suggests this key "gateway" question: *"Why are we considering the alliance? Are we sure that the reasons for engaging in this discussion are based on a recent organizational analysis and planning process, or is it driven by fear? Do we have an accurate read of the environment and where we fit in?"* (McCambridge and Weis, 1997, p. 13).

For those less familiar with *strategic planning*, the term denotes the process that many nonprofits use to examine their vision, mission, and values and to realign their services with the environments in which they operate. Basic components of strategic planning:

- Environmental scanning to identify trends that will influence the future of the organization
- Review of (or creation of) vision, mission, and value statements in light of the future context
- Analysis of opportunities and threats and strengths and weaknesses to define the organization's specific strategic position
- Determination of strategies, goals, and objectives to define the organization's preferred future

My purpose here is not to explain how to do strategic planning. There are already many very solid resources available that instruct nonprofit leaders in that effort. There are, however, aspects of that process that, with a bit of broadening, can contribute to an organization's ability to answer this central question: *Given the specific environment in which we operate, can we more effectively deliver on our mission statement by working together with one or more partner organizations, or by working alone?*

Understanding Your Organization's Unique Environment

As noted, the first step in strategic planning is scanning the environment. Each organization must determine the degree to which its ability to accomplish its mission in the future (say, the next three to five years) will be affected by the changes in its local environments and in its particular field of service (or industry) in addition to other relevant changes. This assessment of environmental fit can be undertaken by executive staff or the Board's Strategic Planning Committee or a combination of both. There are four areas of significant potential change that are most likely to indicate opportunities for consolidation:

- Significant changes in consumer demand or access to consumers
- Anticipated major shifts in current funding patterns

- Substantial changes in the knowledge base (technology) of the service arena
- Actions of other agencies and organizations in the area

Board and staff can become more knowledgeable about each of these by following the steps suggested in this section. The information can be gathered by a Board committee, by staff members, or by a cooperative effort of both.

When you begin such an assessment, it is useful to interview representatives of local foundations to find out what trends they see as likely to influence their giving in the next five years, and to explore their views of the likely changes in your field as well as gaps in services or important issues in your service arena. Key questions include whether the foundations see the need to reduce the number of nonprofits operating in their service arena, and also whether they see opportunities for organizations like yours to work more effectively with others.

You might interview the leadership of other organizations—both those that you interact with on a regular basis and those that work in your service arena without any formal interaction with your organization. Here, the goal is to assess what they see as critical issues for their own planning as well as what they view as the reputation and effectiveness of your services. Ask whether they are seeking partners and for what kinds of initiatives.

Interview representatives of all government entities with whom your organization does business. Solicit their views as to how service funding will change in the next five years. In particular, find out if they plan to reduce the number of nonprofit contractors with whom they do business. Find out if introducing models based on managed care is of interest to them.

For background information, conduct on-line searches of relevant journals, newspapers, and professional publications to identify future trends and issues. If there is a national organization that serves your organization, find out what the national staff are saying about the future. Are they urging increased collaborative efforts among the members? Are they worrying out loud about the survival of smaller members? If there is a support group for Executive Directors in your service arena (the equivalent of a local trade association in the for-profit world), what are the hot topics? Is the support group thinking about moving its emphasis from support to joint initiatives?

It often is not enough to look outside your organization for insight into its environment and possible future. You might want to survey or conduct focus groups among your own professional staff to find out what they are reading, learning at conferences or training sessions, and hearing from colleagues or professional societies. How do they view the continued relevance of your organization as they look to the future? What do they see as issues? Do they feel that the base of knowledge underpinning your services is changing? Are cross-disciplinary approaches to treating your consumers becoming the norm?

In addition, it is useful to visit with consumer advocates if there are any in your field. What is the current status of consumer empowerment? What models are emerging to partner with consumers? What feedback mechanisms are in use? How do consumer advocates define the service continuum in the future?

From your search of professional journals and discussions with staff, what kind of evaluative activity is going on in your field? How important is outcome measurement to funding sources? How difficult is outcome measurement?

Analyzing the Scan Results

A key piece of analyzing the information you raise through the scan process is determining the relevance of the *conceptual base* of your organization and the competencies that will be needed for the future. (The conceptual base is the knowledge or know-how on which your services rest, "the way we do what we do.") Through innovation, conceptual bases change over time. Innovation can be categorized in one of two ways: the *breakthrough,* that is, the invention of a process or product that replaces the previous version as the CD replaced the phonograph record, or the *hybrid,* the blending of technological knowledge from previously separate fields as the marriage of optics and electronics yielded optoelectronics, the source of fiber-optic communication systems (Kodama, 1992).

Our nonprofit sector, working in breakthrough mode, has replaced orphanages with group homes and poorhouses with welfare subsidies. In hybrid mode, we've begun to apply graphic arts training to the problems of teaching children critical thinking skills and problem solving and to use the performing arts to teach teamwork. Our increasing knowledge of brain chemistry has brought on the veritable collapse of our old knowledge bases of health, mental health, and substance abuse. Child Opportunity Zones—which bring together education and social services—also illustrate the hybrid innovation process in action, as does the vast increase in multidisciplinary services for the homeless, for the dually diagnosed, and for families with complex issues.

In this way, then, the ideas on which an organization is based pass through a curve that is remarkably similar to what managers in the for-profit sector will recognize as the classic product demand life-cycle curve. There is a stage of latency or emergence, followed by accelerating growth—with a peak at maturity, followed by decline. Figure 1.1 illustrates the process.

The particular curve in the figure is certainly not inevitable—some concepts die an early death and some stay current for a very long time indeed. The model says nothing about the chronological duration of the curve, only that it exists.

As mentioned earlier, the concept base that led to the establishment of orphanages is a set of ideas that has faded from the pantheon of program models. It has been replaced by concepts that foster smaller group home settings, efforts at family reunification, a wide range of counseling programs and economic support programs, parenting courses, and so on. In fact, as a society, we simply don't regard the care of children whose families have problems in the same light we did even one generation ago. The technology has changed. We also don't put people with mental health problems or developmental disabilities in large warehouse-like institutions. Such institutions as are left are considered

Figure 1.1. Conceptual Base of Organizations.

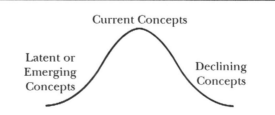

Current Concepts

Latent or
Emerging
Concepts

Declining
Concepts

dinosaurs and are slated for dramatic reductions in size, if not out-right closure.

In some cases, such shifts will force an organization to rein-vent itself. Action for the Environment is the largest environ-mental group in a three-state region. It was founded twenty years ago and has a membership base of five thousand households. The organization has been led by a series of dynamic and charismatic individuals who, through a combination of force of personality and organizational commitment to high-quality research, have positioned the organization as a primary adviser on environmen-tal issues. Representatives are usually first on the list to be invited to high-level discussions of changes in environmental policy or for consideration of environmental impact of specific projects. Critical to being at the table with policymakers is doing your homework—that is, staying one step ahead in knowledge about your field. In this way positions are always well informed and based on high-quality facts.

As a result of the last twenty years of effort, pollution problems in the region served by Action for the Environment are now rarely caused by isolated incidents of poor judgment or neglect. The organization's leadership has recognized that in the future the major issues will center on what the great collective of residents do. Recycling, runoff from septic systems, sewage treatment, acid rain, product packaging, electricity consumption, use of automobiles—all are examples of the future issues of environmental action. None of these issues can be dealt with by galvanizing a hundred pickets to show up at the statehouse or in front of a business that is dump-ing wastes. New methods to influence the private actions of many individuals scattered throughout the area will be required to cope with these larger systemic issues. The leaders of Action for the Envi-ronment are now exploring community development models as the next technology for environmental advocacy.

Determining the answer to this question of continuing rele-vance of the concept base is important for all organizations—but it is particularly important for small, weakly funded organizations, simply because keeping competencies current can be expensive. So if your organization finds that the concept base of your services is on the declining side of the curve, you may have discovered an opportunity to work with others to overcome this problem.

The Relevance of Your Management Model

In your assessment, you may discover several ways in which expectations of the management of your nonprofit will change. The following list touches on some of the more common change points that a variety of nonprofits are experiencing. Clearly not all wiil be relevant to every organization and your analysis may have others to add that are unique to your field.

- *Cost-effectiveness:* A combined expectation of low cost and high quality.
- *Evaluation of outcomes:* The ability to demonstrate the connection between an organization's actions and an effect on a consumer or a social problem.
- *Quality assurance:* The design and implementation of a variety of consumer feedback mechanisms to assess service quality on a continuous basis.
- *Tracking:* The ability to establish and maintain a sophisticated system of information to track and analyze outcomes and financial data.
- *Collaboration:* The ability to work with other organizations to accomplish system integration, reduce cost, or create multifaceted interventions.
- *Social impact:* The ability to influence public policy debate on systems change.
- *Increasing dependence on fundraising:* Increasingly sophisticated fundraising methods that build and maintain donor loyalty.
- *Adaptability:* The ability to design and redesign how the work of the organization is accomplished in response to major environmental changes.
- *Enterprise:* The ability to start and manage for-profit initiatives.
- *Outreach:* The expectation that your organization will interact with its consumers in new ways, perhaps shifting power to natural networks for consumer support or providing increased consumer control over shaping of services.

In the substance abuse field, for example, small agencies have been particularly hard hit by changes in management expectations. Substance Abuse Services is a small incorporated agency located in a rural area. It has provided substance abuse counseling since the 1960s using a combination of volunteer crisis workers and professional staff. In the last five years, it has successfully negotiated contracts with surrounding school districts to provide on-site workers at area high schools. While the organization receives small municipal appropriations from the four towns it serves, covering part of the cost of providing services to the uninsured, the number of clients who cannot pay has climbed steeply. Simultaneously, the number of insured clients has dropped by an almost equal degree. Recently, the Board recognized that it would face bankruptcy within a year if the agency could not find additional sources of revenue.

In their scan of their environment, the Board members discovered that only the largest substance treatment agencies are able to compete for consumers who can pay for services. They do this by spreading overhead over a large number of clients, by offering a wide array of services such as detoxification and residential and outpatient treatment, possessing sufficient capital reserves to deal with capitated rates, and installing sophisticated management information systems that can track outcomes. While the Substance Abuse Services programs are of high quality and are still very much needed in the communities the organization serves, management requirements for the services it offers may yet put the organization out of business.

In summary, then, we can see how the technology of *managing* social purpose institutions is changing, increasing in complexity to such a great degree that, in a number of fields, it requires the resources of major organizations with complex infrastructure to accomplish. If this is the case in your field, you can turn the growing recognition into an opportunity to work with others to overcome the problem together.

Need for Additional Competencies

It is helpful if you summarize what your organization needs by way of individual skills and collective competencies and think through what it is you need to do to acquire them. You can fill the gaps by several means: hiring staff with requisite skills and experience, retraining existing staff, partnering with other organizations, and obtaining grant funding for pilot projects.

In determining your approach, remember that many of the competencies your organization acquires may need additional supports in the form of computer technology, facilities, and so on, besides the initial cost. Once the Board or executive staff have determined the need for new competencies, it is necessary to think through the logistics of how the organization will get and keep them. Here too, opportunities to partner with other organizations can be found.

Availability of Slack Resources

You may also identify excess capacity that could be made available to another organization. In your assessment, consider physical plant, cash or investments, program expertise that can be shared or taught, administrative systems capacity, and political expertise and influence. It is much simpler to arrange mutual assistance— that is, to trade excess capacity in one area for what you need in another—than to develop a joint venture wherein you and your new partners seek something you all need and none of you have. The latter can be accomplished, of course—but it's much simpler when you're building on a foundation of trust laid down by mutual assistance than when you're working from scratch.

Existing Strengths and Weaknesses

Another critical strategic planning step is the analysis of strengths and weaknesses in your organization's current base of programming (what the for-profit world would call your product or service lines). This assessment should yield the answers to the following questions:

- How well do our programs fit with our vision and mission?
- What is the relative competitive strength of each of our programs?
- Do we have programs capable of growth in the environment as we envision it?
- Are we engaged in any services which, if eliminated, would cause consumers irreplaceable loss?
- Should we work with another organization to sustain a service or pursue an opportunity?

The MacMillan Matrix is a tool that The Support Centers uses to help nonprofits answer all these questions. A copy of the matrix and a brief explanation of its use is included in Appendix A. More detailed instructions are available in *Strategic Planning for Nonprofit Organizations: A Practical Guide and Workbook,* by Mike Allison and Jude Kaye.

Whether you choose to use this tool or not, it is a good idea to take an objective look at your organization's programs. The ones that fit the three patterns listed here offer the best opportunity for working with other organizations:

- Programs that are weakly positioned against competitors but fit with the organization's mission and vision. You might believe that these programs are critical, but they may not be sustainable without help.
- Programs that are strongly positioned against competitors but lack essential resources or key competencies within your organization. A partner might be able to fill the gaps.
- Programs that are the dominant services in the region— that is, the ones that serve the most consumers, provide unique or especially high-quality services, or are particularly cost-effective in delivery. You might be able to expand these programs by picking up weaker, less-well-positioned programs of other organizations.

This issue of shifting program relevance and sustainability is of particular importance for traditional social welfare agencies serving indigent populations. The federal government has slated block grant consolidation for several funding streams that have sustained this programming in recent years, and—through welfare reform— many states are reconsidering their commitment to this population. The following example shows how one such agency analyzed its programming.

Community Action, Inc., operates with an annual budget of $4.3 million and provides services to low-income individuals and families. Its catchment area includes very-low-income semi-urban communities with a high proportion of refugees, single-parent families, unemployed and underemployed people, and also some middle-class suburban households.

Services currently include a wide array of basic needs supports: food, clothing, shelter assistance, a range of services to support the elderly, a day care center serving three-to-five-year-olds, and a community health center. The organization sponsors a very strong volunteer program.

The conceptual base of Community Action is embedded in providing relief of suffering among the poor through a wide range of direct supports as well as assisting individuals and families to access government benefits for which they are eligible. While this conceptual base will have continuing relevance—there will always be individuals who are chronically dependent due to illness, age, or disability—there is a significant societal change in attitude toward dependency. This change couples relief of suffering with the expectation that an individual or family will take action to move toward self-sufficiency as soon as possible.

The Strategic Planning Committee has identified several areas where the agency has the ability to start new programming. Each will require a significant degree of investment. As the committee sees it, there is already a significant unmet need for infant and toddler care, and the need for after-school programming for older children will grow with welfare reform. Welfare reform also means that the community will need social service programming that emphasizes self-sufficiency. Due to the agency's strong relationship with the population receiving welfare support, staff members believe that there is also an opportunity to integrate job development into their existing service base. In addition, there will be an increased need for case management services for the elderly—but the state has already announced its intention to put these services out to bid as a single contract within two years.

While the Strategic Planning Committee sees all these opportunities, the agency presently has the resources to invest in only one. In addition, the provision of health care has changed so dramatically in the region that the agency can no longer provide health services to uninsured clients. The Strategic Planning Committee fully recognizes the importance of these services to indigent people but the agency cannot manage the growing deficits in this program. It must either find another organization able and willing to share this burden on behalf of the community or close the program. We will return to Community Action later in this chapter and again in Chapter Two to follow up on what the organization did in response to these insights.

Consolidation and the Board of Directors

If the Board of Directors has not already been involved via a committee in the activities outlined thus far, this is the time to engage the Board members in the ongoing discussion as to whether consolidation is a choice that the organization will pursue. The first step is to educate the Board about the organization's overall strategic position so that there is a complete context for making any decision about pursuing partners. This summary statement—sometimes called a *situation assessment*—includes the following components:

- A statement of the organization's vision, mission, and values
- A brief synopsis of recent strategic decisions
- A listing of high-priority trends to which the organization will probably have to respond
- A statement of relevance of the current conceptual base
- An analysis of current programming
- An analysis of potential new programming
- A statement of needed competencies for the future and options for acquisition

The document capturing the assessment should be provided to the entire Board. If consolidation options have been identified, and if there are choices to be made, this is best accomplished with significant Board involvement.

Continuing with the example of Community Action, the Strategic Planning Committee identified four programmatic priorities. After reviewing the committee's findings, the Board decided that all the options should be pursued. After a thorough discussion of each, they placed the options in chronological order, recognizing that external factors would at this point be a strong influence on their ability to accomplish their goals. Here's what they came up with:

Priority 1. Elder case management: The Department of Human Services has strongly indicated their intent to put these services out to bid as a statewide contract within two years and has stated their preference that some of the existing providers create an entity capable of bidding on the contract. Existing staff and the strong volunteer component will make CA, Inc., an asset in the emerging system.

Priority 2. The Health Center: This facility is in such serious disrepair, and the financial situation is sufficiently bleak, that pursuit of a partner to assist with the situation will have to be undertaken concurrently with the creation of an elder case management consortium.

Priority 3. Job development: This initiative will be pursued after the first two are well underway, because it is unlikely that welfare reform legislation will pass within the next twelve months. The agency has some funds to invest in this. A further feasibility study will have to be undertaken to determine whether or not the agency will need a partner.

Priority 4. Infant/toddler program: Extension of the day-care facility will require submission of grant proposals to a number of sources. The most likely source will be municipal Community Development Block Grant Funds. The grant cycle for these funds will not begin for another six months. The agency expects to be able to raise the funds for this project, but may wish to look for a partner with expertise in this type of programming.

Next Chapter

In Chapter Two, we will explore the process of readying your organization for negotiating around the specific opportunity you have identified, including the groundwork for the search for partners. For most organizations, this will be the first time that the Board and senior management have had to work together in a process with such complex dynamics. Taking the time to establish clear roles and responsibilities and to frame needed policies will pay off in reduced confusion and the ability to communicate with one voice. Staff must also be prepared to understand and accept the path the Board has chosen. Where the specific partner has not already been identified, there is also thinking that must be done ahead of the actual search.

Chapter Two

Preparing for Organizational Change

We will move forward from this point assuming that your leadership has decided that consolidation is an appropriate strategic option. Before beginning pursuit of a specific partner, it's a good idea to address the issue of organizational readiness.

Preliminary Planning

There are fourteen separate steps listed here—which may seem like a lot at first glance. However, even those with a low tolerance for process will find them useful, no matter how impatient they are to get down to the business of negotiation. These steps will help both reduce and deal with the internal conflict that is almost certain to arise over plans to restructure an organization. One of the unique aspects of managing a nonprofit is the need to balance the needs and preferences of its multiple stakeholders, all of whom tend to be value-driven individuals. Care taken now will pay off later when the organization is faced with serious and definitive agreements to be ratified.

1. *Make sure that internal constituencies understand at least the broad outlines of your organization's situation in the environment.* Any option that involves corporate restructuring will increase ambiguity for some staff and Board members. Before you go forward, nearly everyone involved should be able to state, succinctly and correctly, the relative position of the agency in its environment. It is always helpful to people facing major organizational changes to have a well-defined context for viewing the proposed change. If

the proposal makes sense given the organization's position, it is more likely that internal constituencies will accept it and support it—though this will not necessarily take away their anxiety. A strongly stated situation assessment can help.

2.   *Identify one or more goals that leadership would like to accomplish as a result of consolidation. State these goals clearly in terms of outcomes.* The Board of Directors and management must be very clear about what it is that they are trying to make happen. The more precise you can be, the better—nothing will doom discussions more quickly than sending the message to a potential partner that you aren't quite sure what you want.

Here are some examples of useful goal statements:

- We are seeking one or more strategic partners to share in the responsibility for designing, financing, and managing a facility that will serve as a performance venue for dance companies in the region.
- We are seeking one or more partners to share the costs of management infrastructure necessary for continuing growth, specifically an integrated billing and quality assurance management information system.
- We are seeking one or more partners to design a vehicle by which we can collectively compete for managed care contracts on a statewide basis.
- We are seeking a partner with an existing continuum of services into which our services can be fully integrated.
- We are seeking substantial partners who share our intent to take the lead in setting standards for our service field in this region and will work with us to influence state officials in the design of new service systems.
- We are seeking a merger partner who will guarantee our professional staff at least one year's employment from the date of consolidation.
- We are seeking a merger partner who will guarantee that [name] program will be kept intact for at least three years from the date of consolidation.

3.   *Determine the degree to which these plans have the support of the Board, management, and key staff.* There should be a fairly strong

consensus among the organization's leadership that you have a goal worth pursuing. It becomes more and more important as these processes unfold that the organization speak with one voice. Negotiating with potential partners becomes close to impossible if there is bickering going on internally as to whether your organization should be engaged in the process at all.

Do not be surprised by the depth of Board and staff member emotions that surface in the process. Even at this early stage, it is likely that individual Board and staff members will have strong feelings about what is occurring. Potential loss of autonomy or the suggestion of sharing control with another organization can be very frightening. Most people recognize that these situations will require new behaviors and perhaps new knowledge on their part. Expect that insecurities will show themselves and recognize that they may appear as acting out rather than as direct expressions of emotion. It is critical for leadership to convey confidence that what is occurring will be a further expression of the organization's mission. Tapping into the strongly held values of Board and staff can be very helpful in calming anxiety and assisting individuals to see what may be personally upsetting news in a larger, more positive context. Remember that people may need to be shown in some detail how the chosen strategy will enhance mission. It is impossible to talk too much about this.

4.   *Determine the degree to which these goals have the support of key funders, key donors, important political supporters, existing collaborative partners.* Leadership should check in with these important external constituencies to assess their reaction to the proposed initiative. While many funders have developed policies to deal with the potential consolidation of their grantees, others have not. This is not to say that the initiative should be abandoned if a key constituent has objections. Rather, this check-in process will identify constituents who may cause problems later on and will allow leadership to pinpoint who needs to be further educated. This effort can also yield important information that may legitimately reduce a Board's willingness to go forward—for example, if a state department or municipality says that it will pull a contract if an organization merges with a particular partner or if it merges at all, the plan might not be beneficial no matter how many other advantages it offers. At the least, you will discover which external constituencies feel that they must approve what your choices are.

5. *Educate Board and management about their options for accomplishing what they wish to do.* The leaders of most nonprofits do not have the knowledge base to make sound decisions about options for restructuring without help. Set aside time to share helpful materials or engage outside consultants—or both—to provide an overview and context for understanding the options that may soon be under discussion with a potential partner.

6. *Carefully think through the potential impact on the organization if the initiative succeeds.* While all the possible effects of success cannot be anticipated, many can. Who will be most affected? What is the range of possible effects on these individuals? Whose self-interest may be undermined or injured? Are those who may be injured in key decision-making positions? What checks are in place to ensure that these decision makers do not use their own self-interest to influence the negotiating process? This is especially important if the CEO's job may disappear or change radically. If that is the case, Board leadership must take care that the success of the negotiations does not rest entirely on the CEO's continuing good will.

If specific senior managers are likely to lose their jobs as a result of the planned consolidation, the Board of Directors may want to consider negotiating a formal agreement that these individuals will stay in place until the consolidation is complete. Such statements are called *key employee severance agreements.* In return for agreeing to carry out their duties and not resign during the negotiations, these individuals may be guaranteed severance pay or benefit continuation for a length of time. The specifics of these agreements will depend on the degree to which keeping these individuals in place is critical to the ongoing operation, the seniority or length of service of the employees, and the degree to which each employee's support of the negotiating process is needed. Clearly Board leadership must take great care that the actual financial resources exist to keep these agreements once the consolidation has occurred. Note that the legal term for these agreements is an *agreement and general release* and that the actual documents should be drafted by an attorney. (The issue of the CEO's role in negotiating a future position is discussed more fully in Chapter Nine.)

7. *Determine the amount of funds available to pay for the professional services that will be needed to support the process.* How much can the organization tolerate losing if the process fails? It is highly unlikely

that consolidation will be accomplished without the aid of an attorney, and there may well be other expenses. Recognize that there will be costs and there will be risk. For example, a small organization was approached by a very large organization for a possible merger. The small organization was not opposed to these discussions. The larger organization forwarded a copy of a draft agreement that the Board of the smaller organization did not like. The larger organization suggested that the smaller have their own attorney draft something. They did so—but then the larger organization withdrew the offer (for their own reasons). The smaller organization was left with a bill for $3,500 in legal fees and no agreement. (See Chapter Eight for guidance in working with professional advisers.)

8.   *Identify clear parameters and roles and responsibilities for internal and external communication in the search for partners and in the early negotiations.* Early identification of spokespersons will save much time and aggravation later. The protocol of communication within these processes can be critical to success. Many communities are small and Board members of parties to the negotiation may interact socially. Stress the confidentiality of the materials exchanged and persuade Board and staff of the importance of controlling information until a definitive agreement is reached. The first agreement with a potential partner should be how the discussions will be described to employees and other stakeholders. As negotiations proceed, include discussion of how the developments and conclusions reached at each stage will be shared with employees and other constituencies of the potential partners.

9.   *For each opportunity, determine the negotiating team.* Not all negotiations require the direct participation of Board members. Some joint ventures will be entirely in the hands of the CEO to negotiate. While there are no real rules, Board members should be involved in the negotiations when there is a potential to change the corporate structure, changing the governance model and putting the CEO's position into play, and when the risk if the venture fails is significant in relation to the assets and management sophistication of the organization.

However, it is wise to identify a negotiating team to be involved in the process from the outset. This can be an ad hoc committee made up of individuals with relevant experience or expertise, or the president can designate one of the standing committees—the Executive Committee, Finance Committee, or Strategic Planning Committee—or the executive staff. Among the Board members of most nonprofits, there are almost always individuals with what I call "good hearts," that is, with a heartfelt attachment to the mission of the organization. Such individuals can be very passionate about the organization, and, by their participation, will help ensure that the focus stays on your mission. While they may not hold leadership positions, they are very valuable additional members of a negotiating team.

10.   *For each opportunity, define what your organization brings to the table.* It is helpful if the negotiating team identifies the full range of positive attributes that your organization offers a potential partner. In this way, you will go forward, hopefully, from a position of strength. Exhibit 2.1 offers a series of lists that can form the basis of this consideration. Your organization may also have other important strengths that you can add to the ones shown here.

11.   *Establish clear roles for partner identification and early phases of negotiation.* Table 2.1 lays out the basic responsibilities and allocates them among the Board president, CEO, senior management, and the appointed negotiating committee. The table also indicates the points at which the entire Board is involved in discussion or approval. This table is a normative model, that is, it assumes a good working relationship among the president, Board, CEO, and senior management. It also assumes that the organization's leadership supports the consolidation effort and that the planned effort has some restructuring potential. It is an example, not a rule.

In other circumstances, the allocation of responsibilities will differ according to the particular sensitivities in the situation. For instance, if a merger is proposed and the CEO opposes the discussions, Board members will assume all the listed responsibilities. For joint ventures for which there is no possibility of corporate restructuring, executive staff may handle the entire process.

In planning for this stage of the overall process, you will save a great deal of time and effort by creating a responsibility chart like Table 2.1 for your planned process.

12.   *Determine the initial screening criteria.* Once roles and responsibilities have been established, it is important for leadership to think critically about the criteria by which they will identify and

Exhibit 2.1. Organizational Strengths.

Cash Assets
- Unrestricted funds
- Restricted funds
- Borrowing ability

Board of Directors
- Business skills
- Fundraising ability
- Advocacy
- Political clout
- Social prominence

Administrative Systems
- Management information
- Financial accounting and control
- Personnel
- Grants management

Physical Plant
- Equity in real estate
- Site location
- Ease of conversion to alternate use
- Equity in vehicles

Major Donors—Access and Strong Relations
- Program effectiveness
- Donor recognition program
- Direct personal connections
- Giving history
- Name recognition
- Image, style, and status

Direct Service Volunteer Recruitment
- Size of volunteer base
- Professional coordination
- Recognition program
- Media visibility

Unique Competencies
- Intellectual property
- Staff skills
- Program models
- Service continuum
- Loyal audience

screen potential partners. In part, these criteria may be dictated by the nature of the consolidation effort—that is, there may be only one or two organizations in the region with the competence to work on a particular joint venture. However, these criteria will also be strongly influenced by the values of those in leadership positions. Careful and realistic attention to these criteria can save a great deal of time and energy in searching for partners. In my experience, these criteria will be referenced again and again—so it is helpful to summarize these decisions on a single piece of paper that can be retained as part of the records of the process.

Back in Step 2, we discussed the desirability of specifying precise goals for the prospective consolidation effort. Defining the screening criteria takes off from there. One of the examples we discussed in Chapter One was Community Action, Inc. Its Board identified its elder case management program as the first priority for

Table 2.1. Early Stage Roles and Responsibilities.

	Board President	CEO	Senior Management	Negotiating Committee	Board (Approval)
Determine negotiating roles	X				X
Identify potential partners	X	X	X		X
Develop screening criteria		X		X	
Research potential partners		X	X		
Review research				X	
Profile list of final possibilities		X			
Initial meeting	X	X			
Manage early relationships	X	X		X	
Narrow options	X	X		X	
Internal communication		X	X		
External communication		X	X		
Formal negotiations	X	X		X	
Final agreements				X	X

consolidation. Seeking help to build a statewide system, the Board described ideal partners as having existing high-quality elder case management services that are well respected by state officials. It also wanted partners to be willing to help develop and implement standards and protocols for case management services and to work with Community Action on issues of staff training and quality assurance. Ideally, partners would be willing to use their influence with foundations to secure necessary start-up funds and would be willing to make a significant investment of their own funds in the start-up. A strong commitment to continuing these services and compatible values were also important aspects of Community Action's vision of its ideal partners.

As an initial screening criterion, the Community Action Board felt that previous experience in supporting the independence of elderly people was a realistic place to start identifying possible partners. It realized that there were very few organizations currently engaged in case management and felt it necessary to broaden the screening to include other services to the elderly. The Board then went on to identify its bottom-line criteria, the ones that would enable the negotiating committee to screen a candidate in or out: a common vision and value system based on elderly independence and the importance of case management, a reputation for high-quality services, and a willingness to invest cash up front. These criteria enabled the strategic planning committee to identify candidates and then, once a relationship was established, to determine in fairly short order whether continuing discussions would be worthwhile.

13.   *Identify potential partners.* There are two methods for identifying potential partners. The first is to use the knowledge and relationships that already exist within the organization's leadership. Board members may know individuals employed in senior positions in surrounding organizations who might be open to inquiry. A potential partner might be identified among organizations already collaborating on projects or programs. The CEO may have personal relationships with other CEOs. If these relationships are very strong and the knowledge of the potential partner is very high, leadership may wish to proceed directly to an informal inquiry of interest.

If the potential partner is not known to anyone within your organization, further research can be conducted. Do not neglect to look beyond the borders of your region or state; with the spread of managed care, catchment areas have broadened dramatically. In conducting research you will discover that quite a bit of information about an organization's relative health is readily available. In many states, information to support licensure is public information. Further access to financial information can be obtained by seeking out the latest IRS Form 990 filings, if applicable. (Organizations with budgets under $25,000 do not file this form.) Using the electronic search capability of your local newspaper or public library, it is often possible to review all the press coverage that a particular organization has received in the last two to three years. A more direct approach is to request the annual report from the administrative offices of your potential partner—or drop by and pick up program service brochures or newsletters. You may also wish to inquire among Board members (and more quietly among colleagues) about how a particular organization is perceived. Once you have reviewed the information you can gather from public sources, leadership can proceed to direct contact to explore possible interest in your project.

The second method is to issue a formal Request for Proposals (RFP). Using existing relationships as well as other potential contacts and leads, the negotiating team identifies a list of possible partners. The team then prepares materials describing your organization in the form of an RFP, setting out what it is you are trying to accomplish and the criteria for your ideal partner. Interested parties are asked to send a letter of interest by a specific date. The more formal research outlined in previous paragraphs is then conducted only for those organizations who express an interest. An outline for an RFP appears in Appendix B.

14. *Prepare for when other organizations approach yours.* It is highly likely that if your organization has come to see one or more of the consolidation options as strategically advantageous, other organizations in your area or region are coming to similar conclusions. The Board of Directors must decide how to handle any approaches that occur. It is useful to think through a decision tree to govern these situations, essentially a response policy.

Figure 2.1 provides an outline for such a process. The model presented here is one that was developed by a nursing home. It is not a recommendation, just an example—followed by a point-by-point discussion of what was considered in coming to the conclusion reached. Every organization will differ in its own assessment of

Figure 2.1. Sample Response Policy.

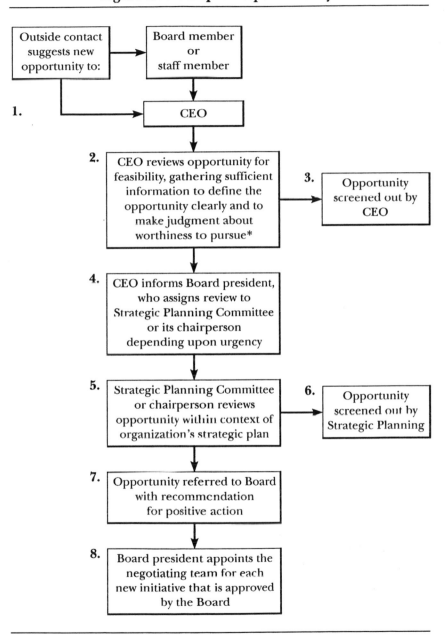

*CEO must gain approval of the Board president or Strategic Planning Committee if significant agency resources are required to test feasibility at this point.

how to handle these issues. Size of administrative staff, knowledge and sophistication of Board members, and resources available to support the process are all variables that must be considered.

The point here is to be prepared with a process that has been agreed upon so that opportunities are not lost while leadership fumbles with whose job it is to do what. As the speed of organizational interaction picks up, the difference between involvement in an important initiative and being left out may depend on how quickly your organization's leadership can make up its mind that it wants to talk about it. The next paragraphs go through the main points in the figure, keyed to the reference numbers.

1.   The suggested model places the CEO or Executive Director as the front line for receiving all approaches from other organizations. These approaches may be made formally or informally. A Board member or a staff member may be approached at a dinner party by the Board or staff member of another organization and may be informally sounded out for receptivity. This model proposes that all inquiries be referred to the CEO for initial screening. Board or staff members receiving such inquiries should indicate nothing to the person making the approach other than that it will be referred to the CEO.

2. and 3.   The suggested model also places the CEO at the first line of testing the potential opportunity for feasibility. As noted in Figure 2.1, feasibility testing may require the expenditure of resources. The CEO may need legal or accounting advice or may need to gather significant data or invest significant time. (The definition of *significant* will vary according to the assets and resources of the organization.) Parameters should be made clear as to the amount that the CEO can expend without involving the Board president or the president's designee. The model gives the CEO the option of screening out an inquiry without further discussion or action.

Some may find that this model gives too much power to the CEO to screen out alternatives that, while in the interest of the organization, may not be in the self-interest of the CEO. If this is a concern, an alternative would be to require the Board president's agreement before an alternative is discarded.

4.   In this instance, if the CEO believes that the opportunity should be pursued, the CEO alerts the Board president. The president then assigns responsibility for reviewing the opportunity to

the Strategic Planning Committee. If there is a tight time frame for responding, the Board may wish to allow the chairperson of the Strategic Planning Committee to give the CEO approval for pursuing the opportunity.

5.   The chairperson reviews the opportunity with the members of the Strategic Planning Committee to determine if it fits within the plan and offers the organization the opportunity to further accomplish its mission.

6.   The model gives the Strategic Planning Committee the option of screening out the opportunity without further discussion.

7.   The Strategic Planning Committee may also recommend the opportunity to the Board for positive pursuit.

8.   The Board president appoints the negotiating team for each approved initiative.

The Board of Directors that adopted this particular model wanted to accomplish several things: (1) to establish clearly defined roles of Board and staff in screening new opportunities; (2) to create a model that would allow for the quick pursuit of opportunities while using Board member time judiciously; (3) to define the parameters for the expenditure of resources on early feasibility testing; and (4) to ensure that new and unexpected opportunities were taken up only when they fitted in with the organization's existing strategic direction. The latter point was particularly important, as the Board recognized full well that pursuit of an unexpected opportunity may be at the expense of a planned opportunity. Appendix C is a worksheet for constructing such a response policy for your organization.

Next Chapter

Chapter Three begins with a discussion of the need to match purpose with structure and introduces four structural models: joint ventures and partnerships, management service organizations, parent corporations, and mergers. The chapter then focuses on joint ventures and partnerships: what they are, how to put them together, tools to help you, and issues related to managing them once they are in place. The following chapters deal with the remaining three models, and the discussion of pursuing partners resumes in Chapter Seven.

Part Two

Understanding Alliance Options

Chapter Three

Joint Ventures and Partnerships

The structure of an organization has a profound influence on the behavior of the people who work within it. Structure doesn't necessarily dictate behavior—but it does influence it strongly. The degree of complexity involved in carrying out your purpose should influence the degree of complexity of the structure you choose. Your future intentions also will influence structure choice; a long or permanent relationship will be structured more formally than a temporary one. In a very real sense, the most important decision that you will make with your partner is the legal structure.

Before proceeding to seek out partners for your new venture, it is wise to educate your own leadership about the range of alternatives that exist for structuring the planned endeavor. Great care must be taken to build a thorough understanding of the implications of the options that are available, as few Board members will be well versed in them. Most CEOs will be aware of one or two and may have actual experience with only one. The natural human tendency to stick with known quantities may well put them at a disadvantage in the negotiations unless they understand the options up front.

The pyramid chart in Figure 3.1 provides a quick overview of the four options. The bulk of this chapter is devoted to joint ventures and partnerships, the most cautious approach to working with another organization. In the chapters that follow, we will look at the other three options for corporate restructuring.

Figure 3.1. Consolidation Continuum.

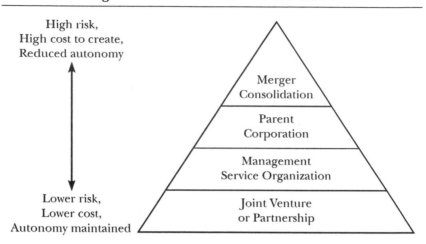

High risk,
High cost to create,
Reduced autonomy

Merger
Consolidation

Parent
Corporation

Management
Service Organization

Lower risk,
Lower cost,
Autonomy maintained

Joint Venture
or Partnership

As you proceed, remember these basic rules of organizational development:

PURPOSE DEFINES STRUCTURE

and

STRUCTURE BREEDS BEHAVIOR

General Approach

In each of the discussions in this chapter and the three that follow, you'll find similar information at a similar point. This will make it easier to compare the relative advantages and disadvantages you can expect to encounter, given your own situation. Here is a brief summary of the perspectives I use to describe the four models.

Basic definition: The terms applied to organizational restructuring are often confused, so I begin with a basic definition that seeks to differentiate clearly among the models.

Best use: There is no one-best-way or one-size-fits-all approach that everyone can adopt. The discussion therefore includes some guidance as to the purposes to which the model is best suited, along with one or more brief illustrations of how the model has been used.

Authority and control: Each model implies different relationships between and even within the participating organizations. The discussion covers the fundamental governance and management issues of each model, with recommendations for its application.

Alignment of mission, values, and culture: Organizations possess personalities that are as unique as individual personalities. Just as when individuals try to work together, organizations find that their differences influence the outcome of their efforts when they seek to work in partnership. Mission, vision, values, and culture capture the organizational personality. This section discusses the degree to which the model requires integration between the partners in these areas.

Necessary documentation: More complex models require more complex paperwork. The discussion lists and describes the content of key enabling documents for each of the four models.

Associated expenses: All the models involve some expenditures. The discussion lists the commonly occurring expenses associated with creating the model—but does not estimate the specific level of expense any given organization will encounter. The actual outlay will vary greatly according to the source of professional advice.

Risk factors: None of the models is without risk. This section outlines the major potential risks associated with each, including implications for antitrust action, labor relations problems, and other areas that may not appear obvious at first glance.

Examples: Each of the models has many possible applications. This section gives descriptions of how a few nonprofit organizations have employed the model under consideration, to give you some idea of the range.

Management issues: Restructuring is never a perfectly smooth and simple process, and each model offers its own probable sticking points. This section outlines the areas that are likely to challenge management in the implementation of the model.

Joint Ventures

A *joint venture* is an undertaking of two or more organizations for the accomplishment of a specific purpose. Joint ventures are often time-limited and narrowly defined. They may employ different types of legal entities:

- *A contractual relationship:* A written agreement between or among two or more organizations defining specific contributions, duties, responsibilities, and dissolution. These agreements are often limited to a specific period of time.
- *A partnership or Limited Liability Company:* A formal, legally recognized entity that defines how power will be shared, decisions made, and so on relative to the joint venture. Usually, partnerships are expected to continue for as long as the partners retain good will.
- *A corporation:* A separate legal entity with its own Board of Directors that may be owned entirely or in part by the sponsors of the joint venture. Corporations that have a tax-exempt purpose may be incorporated as nonprofit organizations. These jointly owned corporations are expected to continue indefinitely.

Best Use

Joint ventures allow a very flexible response to the environment in that a single organization may be involved in several ventures with several partners. The more turbulent the environment the greater the need for these highly flexible responses. They are also useful tools to test the strength of an emerging relationship, a first step in what may be a longer exploration of consolidation. Joint ventures never affect the independent corporate status of the sponsoring organizations, and thus they offer organizations the opportunity to work together without the risks involved in an outright merger. (See Chapter Six on mergers for a complete outline of these risks.)

Generally, these agreements are comparatively easy to exit. While partnerships and jointly owned corporations do not have a specifically defined life span, agreements concerning dissolution are generally included in the documents that set up the structures. This ability to pull out of a venture, coupled with the corporate independence of the parties, can be especially important for organizations with very different cultures, who may not work together well at all at very close proximity but who may need or want to try to work together on a specific program or project.

There are many ways to describe the range or types of joint ventures. From the perspectives of nonprofits, the most useful may be a typology that organizes the various types of joint venture by motivation, that is, by what they are trying to accomplish. In the nonprofit sector, the following are among the most common purposes for creating joint ventures:

Knowledge sharing can occur when two organizations recognize that each has a distinctive competency, innovative approach, or specialized knowledge that, if shared, will contribute to higher quality service outcomes for both.

Market access, the ability to bring services to people who have not been reached by previous efforts, can be achieved or increased through joint ventures. At the most basic level, it enhances market access for organizations to simply share their mailing lists. More formal audience development efforts might range from sharing an outreach worker to creating joint public relations materials such as brochures or newsletters to extending a particular service offered by one partner to a special population with whom the other partner has a unique relationship. By sharing program models with a partner, an organization can also accomplish wider geographic reach.

New product or program development is often difficult for a single organization to finance. Increasingly, nonprofit organizations find access to capital is a major impediment to developing new products and programs. As the foundation world responds to the same set of trends as the nonprofit world, funding for research and development into new approaches is harder and harder to find, and the expectation for collaborative effort is increasing. The joint venture model allows organizations to share resources in the development of new products or services and to compete for funding.

Authority and Control

As noted, joint ventures can be captured in a number of ways. To clarify the issues of authority and control, we will look at three alternative structures, each of which can be altered in various ways to suit the parties to the agreement (Figures 3.2–3.4).

In this structure, the two CEOs jointly provide oversight of the project. The day-to-day management is by an employee of NPO #1 who reports directly to the CEO of NPO #1. This provides clear lines of accountability and gives one organization the responsibility for

Figure 3.2. Joint Venture Governed by Contractual Agreement.

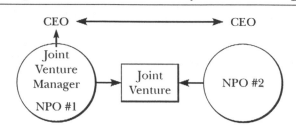

the day-to-day success of the venture. However, both parties to the agreement contribute staff and resources and the CEOs share the strategic management of the venture equally. This is a good start-up model in that it provides a single management voice for staff to respond to. (Start-up is not the time to create ambiguity for the staff carrying out the initiative.)

In this model, the partners have decided to separate the joint venture from their ongoing operations and have set it up with a partnership agreement. They also might use a *Limited Liability Company,* a new form of partnership (explained more fully later in this chapter). Variables that might drive the decision to create this stronger separation from ongoing operations include the decision to operate the joint venture over the long term, the staffing of the joint venture with competencies that exist in neither organization, the sheer size of the joint venture, the need for the joint venture to operate with a different culture (perhaps more entrepreneurial) than either sponsoring organization, or the physical separation of the facility in which the joint venture operates.

In this case, there is a joint oversight committee made up of Board members and the CEOs. The joint venture manager reports directly to the oversight group. This committee would have the responsibility to develop policy for the venture, to evaluate progress, and to keep the respective Boards informed. This model gives the joint venture manager a much higher degree of autonomy in day-to-day operations in that he or she has no regular supervisor (an oversight group that includes Board members will meet only periodically). This model will work if the sponsors have very high confidence in the skills of the manager and very clear expectations for the performance of the joint venture. Deci-

Figure 3.3. Joint Venture Governed by a Partnership Agreement.

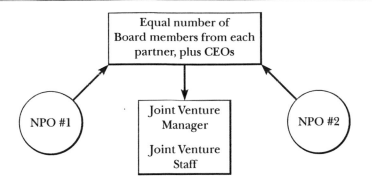

sion making within these types of joint venture oversight groups is most likely to be by consensus and rotating chairpersons are not uncommon.

In this model, the joint venture has been separately incorporated with its own Board of Directors and bylaws. Control of the Board has been assured in the joint venture bylaws by giving a certain number of Board seats to each of the sponsoring organizations and by prohibiting changes to the bylaws without the agreement of the sponsoring Boards. The joint venture CEO will report to the joint venture Board.

If the purposes of the joint venture corporation are tax exempt, 501(c)(3) status can be obtained from the Internal Revenue Service. If the purposes are not tax exempt the new corporation will be run as a for-profit company.

Incorporation of the joint venture should be undertaken if the financial or liability risks are sufficient to cause concern about the protection of the assets of the sponsoring organizations. The decisions relative to which form is most effective will depend on the following factors:

- The degree to which income from the venture will be considered unrelated business income by the IRS.
- The degree to which the mission of the joint venture is within the mission of the sponsoring nonprofit partners.
- The degree to which the mission of the joint venture will be considered tax exempt.

**Figure 3.4. Joint Venture Incorporated and
Governed by Separate Bylaws.**

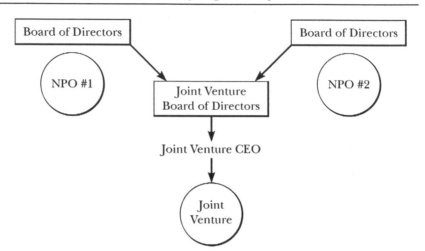

- The specific features of state laws governing the establishment of partnerships and Limited Liability Companies.
- The degree of financial risk. If this is a very risky venture, it is wise to protect the assets of the sponsors by creating a separate corporation.

The specifics of each case will vary and there are no general guidelines. Each joint venture must be examined in light of its own nature and that of its sponsors. Adequate legal counsel is strongly recommended in making these judgments.

Alignment of Mission, Values, and Culture

Clearly, it is not necessary to delve deeply into these organizational aspects if the partners are exchanging resources such as a mailing list or even working together on a single fundraising event—the core corporate structures of the partners are completely uninvolved. As a general rule, if the joint venture is limited in scope as well as in time, that is, if the partners are going to work together for a very narrow purpose for a short period, it is rarely necessary to raise these broader issues of organizational context. When corporate cultures are aligned (similar), negotiations and the ongoing relationship are apt to go more smoothly. (See Chapter Ten for a further discussion of the influence of corporate culture.)

As well, if the joint venture is separately incorporated with its own Board of Directors and management staff, then they are responsible for establishing the new organization's mission, vision, values, and culture. These aspects of the core corporate structures of the partners will influence the formation of the new organization to the degree that they are transferred through interlocking Board or staff members or through the transfer of staff members.

Different cultural orientations among the partners relative to these context issues will cause the most problems in the design stages of more complex ventures and if the joint venture is jointly managed and integrated into the two organizations as in Figure 3.2. This model will require some degree of cultural alignment to work well.

Necessary Documentation

Depending upon the scope of work involved in the joint venture activity, most joint ventures can begin as contractual relationships that are based on a memorandum of understanding or operating agreement. As joint ventures become more complex, the documentation must become more extensive. Incorporated joint ventures should refer to the list of documents in the Management Service Organization discussion in Chapter Four.

Basic Content of an Operating Agreement (Time-Limited Project)

While some individuals may be comfortable committing their organization's resources on a handshake, I strongly recommend that organizations develop an operating agreement (also called a *memorandum of understanding*) for every joint venture, no matter how seemingly simple. These agreements, as well as all the other legal documentation of models described in subsequent chapters, should be viewed as safety nets, tools that will help the parties in case disputes arise. Remember, though, that these agreements cannot substitute for trust, good will, honest intentions, and commitment. Operating agreements should include provisions like these:

- Goals of the project.
- Statement of mission, vision, and values *for the project*.

- Duration of the project, the agreement, or both. (It may be that the joint venture has a potential life of many years, but in its early stages, the agreement may be for one year at a time.)
- Specific responsibilities to be taken by each of the partners in the formation stage.
- Initial financial contribution of each partner and how additional financial contributions will be determined.
- Distribution of any net revenue or loss from the project.
- Commitment of initial staffing levels and how increases or decreases in staffing will be determined.
- Commitment of other services to the project, and arrangement for future contributions if needed.
- Design of governance and day-to-day management structure.
- Initial liability or other insurance issues, if any.
- Schedule and content of expected reporting.
- Designation of a spokesperson for the project.
- The process by which communication to the public or media about the project will be handled or approved.

This agreement should be signed by the Chief Executive Officers of the parties, or, in cases where the CEO does not have the authority to sign contracts (as is sometimes the case with smaller organizations), by the Board president. If sponsors cannot reach early agreement on the issues listed in this section, it is highly unlikely that they will be able to manage any joint project. Thus, in addition to serving as a safety net later in the life of the project, the process of developing the agreement can serve as an early warning system for relationships that will be problematic.

As an example of what you will want to avoid, consider the case of a very young community-based organization that did not yet have its tax-exempt status. The Board of local neighborhood people entered into a joint venture with a larger, more sophisticated agency. They decided to collaborate on a proposal for juvenile delinquency prevention. The idea was that the larger agency would be the fiscal agent for the grant and would gradually transfer the program to the community-based organization as that organization increased its capability. The project ended in utter disaster. The idea of the transfer of control was described in the grant proposal but there was no written agreement on implementation nor was there any agreement on how disputes would be settled.

The first dispute arose over who the project manager actually worked for and, therefore, whose personnel policies would define her benefits, days off, vacation, and so on. Subsequent disputes emerged around her activities and lines of supervision. One of many instances of disagreement occurred when the Board of Directors of the community-based organization became incensed over the project manager's choice of recreational activities with a group of teens—fortune telling with a Ouija board—which they viewed as "seances" and "satanic activity." They discovered, to their horror, that their partner saw no harm in these activities and refused to stop them. As a result of these "value differences," the project manager convinced the larger organization not to transfer control of the project at all. This ended with both organizations damaged, the funding source refusing further money to either agency, the need to return funds that were hard to come by, and so on and on.

Legal Advice and Documentation

In creating longer-term partnerships, the advice of legal counsel will be helpful. Although attorneys can provide options, however, they cannot give you the answer to how you will approach these aspects of your agreement. The solution in each case must be the result of substantive discussion with your prospective partners, confirmed by a written statement. These issues should be included in your discussions:

- The authority of a partner, including duties and restrictions
- Process for making decisions and definition of relative power of the partners
- The degree to which one partner can obligate the partnership without the agreement of the others
- Determination of whether to obtain insurance, and if so, the specific kinds and coverages
- Name and purpose of the partnership
- Definition of all initial contributions including staff time, cash, facilities, services
- Distribution of revenue and losses

- Ownership of any tangible assets purchased in conjunction with the partnership or lent to the partnership by one of the partners
- Tax implications, if any
- How and if other partners can be added
- How the partnership activities will be managed
- How a partner can exit from the agreement
- How intractable disputes will be settled

Associated Expenses

The expenses associated with joint ventures depend on the complexity of the exact format chosen. However, even simple operating agreements should be reviewed by legal counsel. Professional legal and accounting services will be necessary if the joint venture becomes a separate entity.

Risk Factors

Joint ventures and partnerships are governed by conventional rules of responsibility. That is, once you set up to provide services to the public, people can legitimately expect you to do a competent job of it. Incompetence is subject to civil action against the partnership on the part of someone wronged by its actions, even if the incompetence is on the part of only one of the partners or employees. Similarly, all parties to the agreement will be held liable for any wrongful act or omission that leads to the personal injury of another or for any intentionally wrongful act committed during the course of business. All these risks can be protected against through liability insurance. Be sure to check if the activities of the joint venture are covered under existing policies of the partners or if additional coverage is necessary.

Joint venture agreements, like any other agreements, can sour despite the best of intentions. Under the Uniform Partnership Act, which has been enacted (with some adjustments) in almost every state, partners in a joint venture may:

- Demand an accounting of the partnership assets by an outside accountant, probably paid for by the partnership itself.

- Take legal action to dissolve the partnership.
- Seek injunctions to prevent illegal acts.
- Request the appointment of a receiver or third party to handle the partnership's affairs during a dispute.
- Sue for breach of contract.

Care must be taken in the framing of the agreement to identify the limits and parameters under which partners to the agreement can create debt for the partnership. Remember that creation of debt is not limited to borrowing from a bank but includes purchasing on credit of supplies or services, as well as signing leases for space and equipment.

Examples

An agency that serves the disabled population, providing services for vocational assessment and placement, developed a joint venture with an organization that specializes in the treatment and recovery of brain-injured individuals. The unique abilities of each allowed the partnership to provide vocational assessment services to the brain-injured and to develop vocational services that were uniquely suited to this small special population. It would have taken either organization a major investment of time and resources to develop the competencies to provide these services on its own.

Three chamber music groups, all with declining audiences, discovered in a jointly conducted audience survey that there was considerable overlap in their audiences. In an attempt to work together to safeguard the audience for chamber music, they initially converted their mailing lists to the same software and developed a single full list, tagged by source organization, to which they all mailed. As a second step, they developed what they called a "sampler" ticket, providing an opportunity for the audience for one group to purchase a discounted ticket to another group's concert. As a third step, the three groups began to coordinate their concert calendars, negotiating concert dates. As a fourth step, the three groups developed a common calendar of events and mailed it to their entire combined audience. In the future, the groups hope to undertake joint fundraising and Board development efforts.

A Parenting Center was developed as an adjunct to a local school district. Rather than duplicating the services that existed within the community, it brought the various service providers together. At first, the Parenting Center served as a clearinghouse for central access to the existing community services. Next the Parenting Center convinced the provider group to share the costs of an outreach worker, who would be employed by the Parenting Center. The task of this individual was to identify at-risk families by working with the teaching, nursing, and guidance staff in the local schools, conduct home visits, and serve as a primary liaison with the service providers. As time went on, the Parenting Center conducted community needs assessments and identified gaps in services. Working with the provider network and acting as an advocate for the providers, the Parenting Center successfully secured funds to widen the range of services to parents.

A broad-based multiservice agency developed a residential program for adolescents with drug and alcohol abuse issues. The purpose of the program was not to treat the adolescent within the residential setting, but rather to motivate clients to pursue and stay in community-based treatment once released. The residential intervention was ten days in length and transportation was provided so the clients did not miss school in the interim. Due to their track record of success, the sponsoring organization was quite successful in marketing this program to private insurers. Using senior program staff as consultants, the organization has been able to replicate the model with other organizations in the same region who then, through joint venture agreements, acted as both sponsors and managers. The new sponsoring organizations provided the start-up capital and developed the site. The original sponsoring organization has been able to expand the geographic reach of a particularly successful intervention dramatically with virtually no cost.

Management Issues

In the early stages of a joint venture it is essential to create clear lines of authority for the representatives on the oversight team. To what degree does each have the ability to commit organization resources to the project and to make decisions that will stick? One of the difficulties that can arise is the varying status levels of partners' representatives. For instance, if one party appoints its executive director and program manager and the other partner assigns its assistant director and a program staff person, it is highly likely the discussion will be distorted by the different status levels unless the Assistant Director has been given clear authority to commit resources and solve problems.

Another challenge in these partnerships is the need to pay consistent attention to managing the several levels of integration that are required for all but the most simple ventures. Kanter, in her 1994 article "Collaborative Advantage," identifies five levels of integration that are necessary for successful partnerships (pp. 105–107):

- *Strategic:* Overall positioning relative to the environment in which the venture operates.
- *Tactical:* Specific and measurable objectives, coupled with the assignment or deployment of resources to achieve those objectives.
- *Operational:* Day-to-day management.
- *Interpersonal:* Planned process of having participating staff get to know each other.
- *Cultural:* Planned processes for increasing understanding of how each sponsoring organization operates and for ensuring that an appropriate culture is established for the joint project.

In my experience, attention to values, service standards, service protocols, and vocabulary is of particular importance for nonprofits. Oversight committees will do well to assign specific responsibility for these leadership functions—and to assess, on an ongoing basis, how well these functions are being carried out.

Developing and maintaining trust is another critical aspect of managing any kind of alliance. Bergquist, Betwee, and Meuel (1995) point out that "covenants not contracts lie at the heart of successful partnerships" (p. 187). They go on to describe the three components of covenants as *information sharing,* an ongoing commitment to lowering boundaries; *goal clarification,* a willingness to engage in ongoing assessment of the worthiness of goals; and *collaborative models for problem solving* (p. 188).

Their in-depth discussion of the dynamics of managing partnerships teaches the importance of active efforts to maintain trust.

They define the dimensions of trust as intention, competency, and perspective. In a completely trusting relationship, the parties will have no doubt of each other's positive intention. There will be no questions as to whether one party will take advantage of another. As well, the parties will value the specific competencies, knowledge, experience, and wisdom that each brings to the table since this is the probable source of the lasting value in the relationship. The third attribute, that the parties share a compatible view of the world and how it works, is particularly important in long-term relationships. Such relationships have to be adjusted as the environment changes. A shared perspective will increase the likelihood of agreement about the need for important transitions.

As the complexity of a joint venture increases, and as resources and risk increase with it, more formal structures will be needed. This does not necessarily mean that any joint venture beyond the basics should be incorporated separately. In fact, one of the most important challenges in managing joint ventures is to determine when the governance structure should be formalized and the pace at which it should be formalized.

As a recommended interim step in the early life of the venture, the day-to-day management should be assigned to one partner to design and implement. This assignment—which generally occurs when the venture acquires paid staff requiring supervision—will avoid major pitfalls such as needlessly delayed decision making, missed opportunities for growth and development, and confusion of lines of authority for personnel working on the venture.

As noted earlier, the joint venture operating agreement or partnership agreement should deal with how the parties will exit from the relationship. Unfortunately, even the best-designed dissolution process can be difficult to manage if one party is leaving because it is disappointed or unhappy—but a poor process makes an unpleasant situation far worse. As difficult as it may be to accomplish, separating partners should make every effort not to damage one another on the way out the door.

Use of the Limited Liability Company

The Limited Liability Company (LLC) is new kind of legal organization in the United States, now available in almost every state.

LLCs are for-profit companies that are similar in many ways to corporations, except that members of an LLC hold ownership in the company in the same way that partners hold ownership in a partnership. Essentially, the Limited Liability Company is a model that takes the best of both worlds from corporations and partnerships. Like owners of a corporation, owners of an LLC have limits on their liability. The form allows for creation of central management, transfer of ownership, and the perpetual existence of the entity. The income from an LLC, however, is taxed only once, as in a partnership. LLC's are governed by operating agreements, not bylaws.

The most important thing to know about the LLC model is why it is an attractive option for partnerships between nonprofit organizations. The simplest answer is that the sponsoring corporations are protected from liability while the complexity of setting up a corporation is avoided.

As noted, the LLC is a new kind of organization. LLCs are never eligible for tax-exempt status. Legal counsel is required to determine whether the formation of an LLC is an appropriate option for any particular venture.

Next Chapter

Chapter Four takes up the management service organization model. Where joint ventures and partnerships tend to focus on programs, management service organizations take on shared administrative functions for two or more nonprofits. They affect the day-to-day operations of the participating groups, and thus involve more intimate ties than joint ventures.

Management Service Organizations

A *management service organization* (MSO) is an entity created by one or more nonprofits to provide management and administrative services to other organizations. The aim of a management service organization is to achieve efficiency and increase effectiveness in one or more management functions. An MSO can take several forms and can provide a very flexible structure to accomplish administrative consolidation.

There are two basic models. The first is created within a single nonprofit with sufficient excess administrative capacity to share with others. A large organization with fully established management systems can often provide higher quality services to smaller organizations on a fee-for-service basis than they could afford on their own. In this entrepreneurial model, the sponsoring nonprofit may choose to maintain the MSO within its own corporate boundaries or may incorporate the MSO as a separate subsidiary corporation. The decision to separate the MSO would occur if the MSO's activities were so substantial that they posed a liability threat or if the income from the MSO's services threatened the organization's exempt status.

The second model is a partnership, similar in structure to the partnerships described in Chapter Three. The purpose of the partnership, however, is limited to administrative functions. When jointly held, the MSO is created as a freestanding entity that provides management services under contract to its owners, and sometimes to others as well. If all the owners are nonprofits, the IRS may grant the MSO nonprofit status, though the owners may also choose the Limited Liability Company as the preferred legal structure. The granting of exempt status to incorporated MSOs reflects an area of IRS decision making that is very much in flux. Previously, if the MSO served no purposes that would make it a tax-exempt entity, it would have to be organized as a for-profit partnership or jointly held for-profit corporation. However, these MSO structures are becoming so integral to the provision of health and human services that the IRS has softened its stand on this issue.

Best Use

Whether integrated or freestanding, management service organizations provide an effective means to reduce unit costs of services by consolidating costly overhead. An MSO can serve as the mechanism by which a number of independent organizations may initially explore consolidation. In some cases, Boards have even contracted for the entire management of agency programs by an MSO. I consider the MSO to be one of the most effective tools to link small organizations and to improve the quality of management infrastructure.

Increasingly, the MSO model is used to conduct third-party contracting and contract management. As state departments seek to reduce the numbers of providers with whom they do business, groups of organizations can combine under an MSO. The MSO, then, holds a single contract with the state government, distributing funds and providing administrative services to support the contract to its owner-members. In this way, MSOs provide services to their sponsors while also serving as a vehicle to market and contract for sales of services. Using an MSO in this way also protects the concept of local governance of services and increases the likelihood that local presence of services will be maintained.

Most MSOs develop a menu of services from which their members and sometimes other organizations can choose. Typically, the MSO menu is drawn from among the following:

- *Personnel management:* Point of entry for staff recruitment and initial screening, staff training program management, benefits

management including joint purchasing of benefits, personnel policy development, payroll and associated record keeping, compliance with laws and regulations.

- *Facilities management:* Oversight of all leases, management of
  real estate, management of custodial operations, repair and
  maintenance of buildings, upgrading and replacement of
  buildings and major capital assets (copy machines, phone
  systems, and so on).
- *Fiscal services, accounting records, audit:* Fully integrated financial
  systems that enable the analysis of programmatic and fiscal
  data—functions can include billing and collections, generation of management action reports, financial statements,
  tracking of financial trends, block bidding of audits, and
  group purchasing of supplies.
- *Fundraising:* Some MSOs aggregate fund development staff
  and efforts from their sponsoring organizations. Specific
  events or fundraising campaigns may be designated to the
  support of the entire network while individual providers may
  contract for support for individual fundraising efforts.
- *Planning:* The MSO may be designated as the site for strategic
  planning on behalf of the network or may provide planning
  services (data analysis, support to Strategic Planning Committees) for individual providers.
- *Contracts management:* The MSO may take responsibility for a
  wide array of contracts, from leases and equipment rentals to
  contracts with third-party insurers. At the point at which contracts with insurers include assumption of some of the risk
  associated with service provision, the MSO itself may need
  state licensure as an insurer.
- *Marketing:* The MSO may conduct market analysis, identifying
  potential prospects and developing communication strategies
  to reach prospects, including public relations and the design
  and production of communication collaterals such as
  brochures. Again, these efforts may be on behalf of an effort
  in which all providers participate, or may be done on a fee-for-
  service basis for a single provider.
- *Quality assurance:* Establishment of quality standards, monitoring, MIS support, support to utilization review efforts, ongoing
  quality improvement efforts, and outcome studies.

Authority and Control

In the first model (Figure 4.1), in which the MSO rests within a single nonprofit, authority over the MSO's operations is clearly within the purview of the executive director and Board of the sponsoring organization. Even if separately incorporated as a subsidiary, the MSO's governance is defined by its corporate parent. The relationship with other organizations who use the MSO's services is a contractual one, usually based on a fee-for-service model.

The menu and pricing of services are driven, at first, by the excess capacity of the sponsoring organization. For instance, a large provider of services for the developmentally disabled installed a computer system with the capacity to track the revenue and expense of fifty separate business entities. This provider needed only three for its own purposes so it made the rest available to a number of other small, freestanding group homes in the region. Once this set of contractual relationships was in place, however, the smaller groups looked to the larger entity for help with additional areas such as quality assurance. The larger provider then expanded its quality assurance capacity to respond to the needs of the smaller groups. In time, the menu of the MSO became driven by the needs of its customers, though it began with a specific instance of excess capacity.

In the second model (Figure 4.2), an MSO set up as an incorporated partnership is governed by a separate Board of Directors whose members, in this case, are chosen by the Boards of the organizations

**Figure 4.1. Integrated MSO Controlled by
One Nonprofit Organization.**

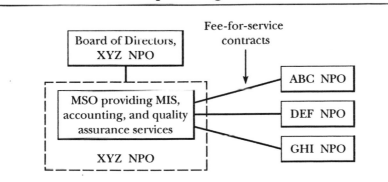

who use the MSO services. The second model is often preferred when the entities are relative equals in that it allows for ownership by all or some of the sponsoring providers. With ownership comes the ability to influence or direct the operation and menu of the MSO.

Generally, an MSO is set up as a service bureau—that is, it does not direct the activities of its members, it serves the needs of its members. In terms of control, members work together to determine the level and definition of quality for the services provided. Members also determine how fees and payment schedules will be set, determine the initial staffing, and so on. This requires a high degree of collaborative problem solving.

MSOs often offer highly sensitive management services. Fundraising, finance, quality assurance, personnel—all of these are areas in which consolidation may be very difficult to undo once the MSO has operated for a period of time. Thus dissolution of an established MSO is often more difficult than dissolution of a partnership that jointly provides programming. I will stress the importance of building these organizations slowly when I get to the Management Issues section later in the chapter, but the point deserves extra emphasis here.

Alignment of Mission, Values, and Culture

An MSO operating under the first model, owned and operated by a single organization, requires no mission alignment among par-

Figure 4.2. Jointly Held Management Service Organization.

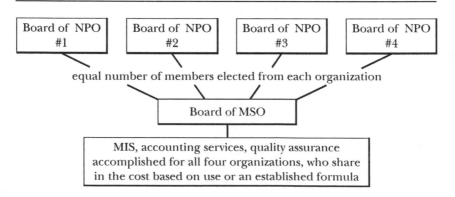

ticipating organizations. Organizations using its services do need to have a baseline trust level to allow another entity to provide these sensitive services—but this is likely to be based on reputation, competence in understanding the contracting organization's data and accounting needs, and ethics.

An MSO operating under the second model is a jointly held business that will be jointly governed by its nonprofit corporate owners. As a service bureau, the new MSO should be built with a "customer service" culture. Because of the working relationship among the partners, this model requires a higher degree of intimacy and harmonious working relationships. While mission alignment is not necessarily a requirement for these relationships to work well, it is important to undertake significant discussions with partners about a wide range of issues and to capture the relative power of each partner within the new organization's bylaws. Alignment around mission, values, and corporate culture becomes critical if the MSO is established as a first step in what is planned as a further future consolidation.

Necessary Documentation

For MSOs operating under the first model, service contracts are the key to survival. The sponsoring organization must pay careful attention to the contracting process as it is this process that will solely define the formal agreement with the organizations the MSO serves. In contracting, the written agreement is ordinarily assumed by the courts to be the *complete* embodiment of the parties' agreement. To be safe—and in most states to be legally enforceable— these agreements should be written in plain and unambiguous language and signed by all parties. This assures that, in case of disagreement over performance, a written document can be produced to settle matters. Most important of all, this practice reduces the likelihood of subsequent disagreement over performance— clearly stated mutual expectations will avert endless rounds of "but I assumed you meant. . . ."

For MSOs operating under the second model, the enabling documents for the independent or jointly held MSO include Articles of Association, bylaws, and a subsequent operating agreement. The Articles of Association will follow the standard format issued by each state's Office of the Secretary of State. Generally, the Articles of Association include a statement of purpose, the names and addresses of the incorporators, the names of the initial Board of Directors, and the date of official incorporation. Bylaws delineate the operation of the MSO's Board of Directors and define membership, terms, meetings, quorum, standing committees, and so on.

Operating agreements are *contracts* that capture the specifics of the ways in which each party will participate in the new corporation. Typical issues covered in MSO operating agreements include the following:

- The specific positions, and sometimes the names of the individuals, who will transfer their employment from their home corporation to the MSO, or how initial staff will be hired
- Site of operations
- Outline of any capital outlay required to set up the MSO and the relative contribution of each party
- The formula (or other agreement) that will be used to share the costs and revenues of the MSO
- The specific functions that will be included in the MSO
- The processes by which individual organizations can "draw down services" from the MSO
- Agreements on name, logo, signage
- The process by which the quality of services provided by the MSO will be assessed
- The process by which disputes will be settled
- The process by which a party may exit from the agreement and the process by which the relative responsibility of remaining parties will be determined should a party choose to exit

Associated Expenses

In undertaking either model, certain expenses are likely to arise. Clearly the actual cost will reflect the hourly fees paid to professional support and the complexity of the documents each model requires. For MSOs operated by a single nonprofit, the service contracts should be at least reviewed, if not actually written, by legal counsel.

For joint MSOs, some organizations choose to use an attorney to file Articles of Association, advise on the creation of bylaws, and to frame operating agreements. Other organizations use consultants or facilitators to develop draft documents that are then reviewed by legal counsel. While some organizations have sufficiently skilled finance staff to develop formulas for distribution of cost and revenue, organizations lacking these competencies should employ a CPA for assistance with this work.

Risk Factors

Whenever one organization enters into a business relationship with another, there is some degree of risk of becoming involved in complex legal entanglements. Care in contracting and in the design of enabling documents can sharply reduce this risk. The integrated MSO, if not set up as a separate corporation by its sponsor, offers no protection for the organization's core business from legal entanglements involving the MSO. The central corporate entity will be subject to the same risks and liabilities as for any other programming. When a single sponsor separately incorporates an MSO, it must be extremely careful to keep the governance and management of the two entities far enough apart to avoid having one corporate entity assume liabilities of the other.

The independent or jointly held MSO offers its corporate owners protection from liability for the actions of the MSO corporation. However, care needs to be taken to control costs in this model. If the parties significantly upgrade their management systems during the consolidation process, costs may rise sharply for some members rather than falling. For instance, if five organizations come together to set up an MSO that will offer public relations among its services, and the two members of the group who had employees specifically assigned to PR work hand off those employees to the new MSO, the remaining three members   who had been dealing with PR on an ad hoc basis—will see their costs for public relations services go up. Meanwhile, public relations costs for the two whose employees went to the MSO will probably go down.

Under either model, an MSO is subject to the same competence expectations and other general liability risks as any other business entity. A freestanding MSO set up as a partnership is also subject to the same risks as other partnership agreements. (See Chapter Three for further discussion of those risks.)

Antitrust Issues

Antitrust considerations only come into play in the application of the MSO model to joint contracting. It is important to recognize that an MSO is not allowed to set prices for services when developing third-party contracts on behalf of a group of providers. For instance, if Blue Cross wishes to put the management of its behavioral health services out to bid to a single contractor, a group of mental health and substance abuse providers can't meet together and agree on a common price and then have the group's MSO bid using that agreed-upon price. To communicate directly concerning the pricing of products and services is considered collusion or price fixing by the Federal Trade Commission and is unlawful. The FTC does allow the use of a "third party messenger" whose role it is to gather pricing information from the several parties and to communicate back to the parties the price that falls within an acceptable range. So the manager of the MSO could gather this information on behalf of the group and then let the group know where the common ground on price is located. Similarly, if Blue Cross is negotiating with a group of providers, Blue Cross may state the rate it wants. The MSO manager then brings this back to the several providers who must then make individual decisions as to the acceptability of the price offered.

The increase in new relationships and affiliations in health care has led the Federal Trade Commission and Department of Justice to recognize the need to issue a formal statement of antitrust enforcement policy or to set out a safety zone for these agreements.

In early January 1997, the two agencies unveiled revised Statements of Antitrust Enforcement Policy in Health Care. The FTC representative stated, "the revised guidelines reflect an effort to protect consumers from unjustified price fixing, while at the same time ensuring that the antitrust laws do not unnecessarily impede development in the dynamic health care marketplace." The policy statements identify a range of provider networks that will not offend the antitrust laws, effectively creating "safety zones" for these entities. Entities that qualify for these safety zones engage in financial risk sharing (such as capitation). For entities outside these safety zones, the FTC intends to analyze whether discussions on price are necessary to make a venture competitive with others of its kind. These agreements on price, however, will be analyzed on a "case-specific" basis. Thus for non-health-related networks the situation relative to the FTC has not yet changed.

On a case-by-case basis, the FTC has asked these kinds of questions in making its determination:

- *Integration:* Do members share substantial financial risk in joint pricing and marketing activity?
- *Messenger model:* Is there a third party conveying information to purchasers? Do individual providers make individual decisions about price?
- *Choice:* What substitutes are reasonably available to consumers for the services in question? Does the network control the market?
- *Market:* Can purchasers contract with other networks? Other providers? To what degree do exclusive agreements impede competition?

Examples

During a community mental health center's strategic planning process, its Board conducted several interviews with Board and staff members of other organizations in the region. It became clear that several important services to the community's overall mental health network were at risk. The area's three shelters: one for the homeless, one for battered women, and one providing transitional living, were each set up as independent 501(c)(3) corporations and were all struggling to stay alive. The mental health center itself had a very strong financial position and very competent management infrastructure including a sophisticated MIS system, human resource director, grant writer, quality assurance program, and other specialized functions. In each of the shelters, the Board was made up of founders of the organization who felt strongly that they did not want to give up their autonomy. By contracting out the management of their organization to the mental health center, the shelters were able to stabilize financially while increasing the competence of their administration. The mental health center furthered its own mission of improving community mental health while gaining some efficiency in sharing its administrative staff with others.

Three visiting nurse services recognized that they could not afford to purchase a sufficiently sophisticated MIS system to compete in the managed care arena as individual agencies. Each was strongly tied to its individual community with a hundred years of history apiece. They established a Limited Liability Company jointly held by the three corporations, combining bookkeeping, billing, MIS, quality assurance, and a twenty-four-hour answering service.

Three small dance companies designed a tiny MSO to share the cost of a single staff person who coordinated all their public relations and handled tours and booking for all three companies. The Board of the MSO was made up of the five company directors.

With the encouragement of a state department of elderly affairs, five providers of case management services to the frail elderly joined together to create a jointly held MSO. They assigned quality assurance, including development of standards and service protocols, to the MSO as a first step. As the service system becomes more cohesive, the plan is for the MSO to take increasing responsibility for administration of the several contracts that the providers currently hold. The state government has announced that it will put these services out to bid as a single contract in two years. At that point, the MSO will serve as the single bidder representing the five current providers.

Management Issues

The greatest challenge in the wholly-owned MSO is to engender a sense of customer service in the staff on the front lines. There is a tendency for people to adopt an attitude that the size and sophistication of their parent organization lets them look down on the small organizations who contract with the MSO. That leads them to provide their information or services in whatever way seems best to them, without regard to the real needs of their customers. This will not bode well for their customer relationships—but at least has a fairly straightforward if not necessarily easily implemented solution.

Issues in jointly held MSOs are more complex. While some health care providers have been forced by the onslaught of managed care to create MSOs very quickly, speed is not advisable and has been the downfall of several. In addition to the management issues inherent in all partnerships and the need to engender a customer service orientation, these new organizations have special challenges that require care and deliberation.

The first arises at the point when employees who were working in the offices of the partners transfer into the MSO. While this is also a challenge in program-related partnerships, the MSO has a special twist. For instance, if the partners have decided that fund development will be the first function to move, this may mean that the MSO will pick up everyone who was previously working in fund development in the partnering organizations. It is likely that these were all one-person offices. Each of the individuals transferring to the MSO may have had full charge of an organization's development efforts. The process of creating a working team may not be easy. However, if the individuals are effectively engaged in considering how the new office can be organized around their individual strengths, competencies, and preferences, the process of integration will be easier.

For each function that is moved to the MSO, a similar and equally careful and inclusive process needs to be designed and carried out. Care must also be taken to ensure that the various function managers do not all come from one of the partners. If all the managers come from just one partner, it may create the appearance of one partner obtaining dominance over the others. Care in these areas will avoid costly disruption of the ongoing efforts of each of the partners and will move the MSO to higher functioning more quickly.

When the function that is consolidated is not as specialized as fund development but is, for example, data entry or basic bookkeeping, staff from the partners may be organized as a pool with all staff contributing to the work of all partners. In this case, it is important to have one individual setting priorities and assigning work so that the several partners will feel that their needs are equitably met and the staff are not beset by divided loyalties.

Another challenge is the temptation for the MSO to drive the sponsoring entities rather than the reverse. As the MSO takes on more responsibility for essential management services, an awkward power balance can emerge. One of the ways the relationship can be kept healthy is the joint determination of performance indicators for the MSO. For each area transferred, the Board of the MSO must create clear objectives that have been approved by the CEOs and Boards of the sponsoring organizations. A well-defined annual operational plan approved by the various Boards will also help keep the MSO's focus on service to its member-owners.

A small number of MSOs have failed because they were designed to serve far more than their original members. In the hope of capturing a share of the administrative market, some partnering organizations have allowed the MSO to take on many functions at the same time and attempt to develop a corporate image of its own in the hope of attracting either additional partners or additional contracts. When the additional partners or contracts failed to appear, the original partners found that they could not sustain what they had built and were forced to dissolve the MSO at great financial loss. While the entrepreneurial model sounds attractive, sufficient capital must be present to sustain the MSO if it experiences early losses. If not, it should not be attempted and the MSO should be built incrementally, piece by careful piece.

Another unique MSO issue is that of the formula for sharing the MSO's expenses. Some MSOs function on a straight fee-for-service basis with an hourly rate devised for each service provided. In the early stages, this is a difficult model to sustain from the perspective of the MSO manager, particularly if each partner pays only for the services used and there is no history on which to base projections. As an alternative, MSO partners often devise formulas that apportion the first year's expenses among the partners, regardless of use. This is another issue where equity must reign. Any appearance of lack of fairness in the design or application of the formula will cause great distrust in the partnership. The variables that go into formula development can be as simple as creating a ratio on the basis of total budget of each of the partners or can be based on a complex set of variables that may differ for each service area included in the MSO. For instance, there may be one formula for facility maintenance that is based on the square footage of space that needs to be maintained and another for fiscal services that is based on the number of financial transactions recorded. The total apportioned expense to any partner will be the result of applying both formulas.

Next Chapter

Chapter Five brings us one step further up the ladder of complexity. Parent corporations are a means of linking separate organizations in a federalist model, balancing the need for central control and local autonomy.

| **Parent Corporations**

A *parent corporation* is an umbrella under which several separate organizations can be grouped. Creating a parent corporation allows people to combine two or more previously separate corporations while allowing them to maintain some degree of autonomy. This model also allows a large and complex organization to divide its activities into units (subsidiaries) in ways that are advantageous.

The corporate parent holds certain specifically designated authority over the governance and management of the corporations grouped beneath it. In our continuum of consolidation—illustrated in Figure 3.1—parent corporations appear just below mergers, because even the most loosely structured parent corporation will mean some reduction in the autonomy of its members.

The new corporate parent exercises its power over the existing corporations via its role as a corporate member, a status that is designated in the rewritten bylaws of the existing corporations. (The concept will be explained in the Authority and Control section later in this chapter.) This model is actually an entire continuum of models since the relative power of the parent and the individual member corporations is a matter of negotiation. Distinct decisions must be reached as to the allocation of responsibility for each aspect of governance and management for each corporate member. In this way, the parent corporation model is an extremely flexible and useful tool, allowing a group of organizations to act as one when that is an advantage and to maintain autonomy when that is an advantage.

Best Use

A parent corporation can be a useful next step beyond an MSO in a phased-in consolidation of two or more organizations.

Remember that an MSO is a service bureau, serving its members. It has no power to compel its members to do anything that the members have not approved. A parent corporation will have some power—and in some cases a great deal of power—over its subsidiaries.

A parent corporation can be used to cobble together a sequence of services that should be integrated on behalf of consumers. This model shows great potential for accomplishing vertical integration of services, bringing together networks under corporate umbrellas. The central parent's primary purpose then becomes fostering and facilitating integration of services. This is an emerging model and offers the opportunity to integrate services while maintaining each nonprofit member's ties to its local constituencies through the protection of the local, individual governing boards. The nonprofit sector is largely made up of organizations with specific local and regional focus. Most representatives will say that they prize their ties to the local communities they serve and are concerned that the creation of mega-agencies that serve enormous geographic areas will destroy that connection. The more loosely structured parent corporation may offer a way to preserve this central value of the sector while allowing organizations to adjust to new market realities.

Since a corporate parent that is the "Sole Corporate Member" of its subsidiaries is considered an owner, this model avoids antitrust issues of price fixing for organizations who wish to bid as a group on managed care contracts. Entities grouped under a corporate parent can fix rates openly among themselves without the use of a third-party messenger.

As noted in the definition, parent corporations can also be useful tools for large, complex organizations who find it advantageous to break their activities into separate corporations. For example, it may be useful to capture all private fundraising activities in a foundation that serves the parent corporation's nonprofit members. Or it may be useful to capture all for-profit activities in a single corporate entity as a subsidiary of a parent. Or to capture a fast-growing set of services that need special handling in a separate subsidiary so as to ensure that they receive sufficient attention or to keep them from drawing away resources and attention from core operations.

Authority and Control

The configuration of authority and control is generically captured in the model shown in Figure 5.1.

However, a parent corporation can also look like Figure 5.2, capturing the functional separation that is discussed in the previous section. A unique aspect of this model is the potential for the various units to purchase services from each other, to share resources, to conduct joint strategic planning, to engage in joint fund development, to seek joint contracting to provide services as a system, and to share in the revenue of entrepreneurial activities from the for-profit subsidiary. (Income from the for-profit subsidiary will be taxed. After-tax revenue can be directed anywhere in the system by the corporate parent.)

Admittedly, parent corporations are complex—complex to understand and complex to put together. To date, it is the larger health care consortiums that have adopted this model all over the nation as a means of coping with managed care. If we can overcome our dislike of complexity, though, it is possible to see how grouping nonprofits in this way can create far stronger entities within the sector, entities that are more efficient by means of shared administrative services and shared competencies, more effective through service integration, and more self-sufficient by inclusion of stronger joint development activities and—where competencies exist—for-profit revenue generation. This can be accomplished simultaneously with protection of a nonprofit's local relationships. In international business, there is a term for organizations that manage to be both global and local at the same time: they are *glocal*. In the nonprofit sector, parent corporations help us to be glocal.

There is another concept that some organizations are experimenting with in conjunction with the parent corporation model, that is, the concept of seeing the corporate parent as "servant

Figure 5.1. Parent Corporation Model #1.

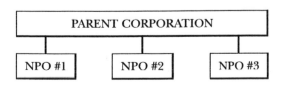

Figure 5.2. Parent Corporation Model #2.

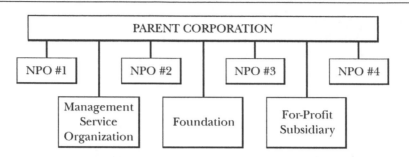

leader." This is a very uncommon approach now but may show potential in time for creating umbrella organizations that are unique in their ability to incorporate nonprofit value systems. Robert K. Greenleaf, in the 1991 book *The Servant As Leader,* speaks of the concept as it relates to the management of a single organization. He says, "The first order of business is to build a group of people who, under the influence of the institution, grow taller and become healthier, stronger, and more autonomous" (p. 30). Some of us believe that this same philosophy should inform the creation of parent corporations in the sector. Used in this way, the parent corporation nurtures its subsidiaries rather than dominating them. This is a teaching, supporting, facilitating, integrating role rather than one of control. This approach is still highly experimental, but intriguing nonetheless. In this model, the configuration of functions might be viewed as shown in Figure 5.3.

Thus, from the perspective of authority and control, *parent corporation* designates not one model but many. This makes it more flexible to use but more challenging to establish in practice as it is essential to make sure that all the participants have the same view of what they're getting into. The agreement concerning the affiliation of the corporations in the group must define its key aspects in considerable detail:

- The goals of the parent corporation formation
- Detailed descriptions of the allocation of governance responsibility, bearing in mind that responsibility may be exclusively that of the parent corporation Board, exclusively that of the subsidiary Board, or shared approvals

Figure 5.3. Parent Corporation Model #3.

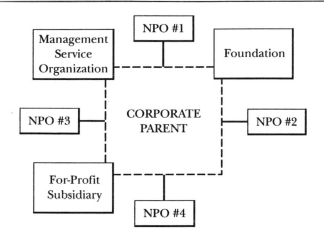

- Definition of how additional members may be added and if and how members can withdraw voluntarily or otherwise
- Terms and conditions for implementing the agreement

How power is allocated within the model depends upon the business realities that will be faced by the new corporate parent and its subsidiaries. In some cases, the degree of integration required by potential funders will necessitate a strong, centrally governed model that will eventually consolidate further into a single merged entity. In considering the allocation of responsibilities in the design phase, participants should identify those areas of management and programmatic initiatives where it is critical for the members to act as one. For organizations faced with shared financial risk in capitated contracts that demand perfect uniformity in protocols and quality assurance, the list of areas where acting as one is imperative will, in all likelihood, be extensive. In that case, most of the governance power will be vested in the parent corporation Board and the subsidiary Boards will retain only advisory powers.

There are other very good reasons, though, why a strong centralized governance structure might wish to protect the existence of subsidiaries and give them some governance responsibility. Maintenance of ongoing relationships with an important donor population may require this. Maintenance of ongoing relationships with an important client population may also require representation from clients on a governing Board. Separate oversight of designated endowment funds may also require maintaining the separate corporation to whom they were given. The name of a subsidiary may have very real value in a particular region.

The least centralized model might allow subsidiaries to use a specific logo, signage, or trademark, or otherwise indicate that the organization is part of a collaborative that adheres to certain standards or uses particular program models or materials. A midpoint might be a parent corporation that is set up primarily to facilitate program integration. The need to create and shape continuums of care for consumers is a task that requires a balance of power between central and local control.

Several specific powers must be allocated within the model. The list given here is not intended to be all-inclusive, nor is it intended to replace legal advice; any organizations seeking to establish a parent corporation should consult with competent legal counsel. Nonetheless, it is useful to look over the basics in advance:

- Control over the content of or changes to the subsidiary's Articles of Incorporation or sections thereof
- Control over the content of or changes to the parent corporation's Articles of Incorporation or sections thereof
- Control over the content of or changes to the subsidiary's bylaws or sections thereof
- Control over the content of or changes to the parent corporation's bylaws or sections thereof
- Selection, approval, and removal of the subsidiary's Board of Directors
- Selection, approval, and removal of the parent's Board of Directors
- Designation of seats on the parent corporation Board for subsidiaries, or designation of seats on the subsidiary Board for the parent corporation
- Appointment power and supervision of the subsidiary's CEO
- Appointment power (or approval) of the parent corporation's CEO
- Control over the name of the subsidiary and its logo and signage

- Financial and programmatic reporting between subsidiary and parent
- Designation of the responsibility for strategic planning for the parent corporation and subsidiary corporations
- Control over endowments, trusts, and real estate belonging to the subsidiary
- Control over the ability of the subsidiary to buy and sell assets
- Control over the ability of the subsidiary to independently declare bankruptcy
- Control over the ability of the subsidiary to incur debt
- Control over the ability of the subsidiary to sign contracts, leases, and so on
- Control over the ability of the subsidiary to enter into collaborative agreements with other organizations
- Control over the ability of the subsidiary to enter into other corporate affiliations, joint ventures, and so on
- Agreement on distribution of the proceeds from joint fundraising efforts, if any
- Ownership and copyright issues for materials that are created by the parent or the subsidiary

Remember that the decisions relative to each item must be reached for each subsidiary. If a group of nonprofits come together to form this new entity, founding nonprofits may have one set of agreements while nonprofits added later may have another. In our functionally structured example in Figure 5.3, the foundation, MSO, and for-profit subsidiary could be given very little autonomy within the system since they exist to support the rest. An instrument that can be used as a discussion guide for these decisions is included at the end of this chapter (Exhibit 5.1).

Alignment of Mission, Values, and Culture

There is a very strong need for alignment of mission, values, and culture for organizations seeking to create a parent corporation. The process of negotiating the allocation of relative responsibility can be onerous, time-consuming, and even rancorous at moments. The parties to the agreement must share a strong sense of accomplishing something that all agree is worthwhile.

It is best to begin the discussions that form the basis of the negotiation with values rather than logistics. If the group does find that its members share values and goals, it will be able to work out the technicalities of the working relationship to suit its members' needs—and it is a very good idea to find out early if this shared set of values cannot be found. People or organizations who cannot reach agreement on a shared vision of what they are trying to accomplish would do well to disband and find other partners before wasting resources at a doomed effort at collaboration. It should be noted that the more power given to the parent and the greater the need for uniform practice across the subsidiaries, the higher the need for integrating the culture of the subsidiaries.

Necessary Documentation

The enabling documents for a parent corporation include four sets of materials:

1. *Articles of Association and bylaws for the parent corporation.* The form for Articles of Association for new corporations (both for-profit and nonprofit) is supplied by each state's Secretary of State office. The form is fairly simple to complete; it asks for the name, official address, and mission of the new corporation, as well as other basic information. Bylaws delineate the rules of operation of the corporate Board of Directors; define membership; describe the method for election of members, officers, and standing committees; and spell out terms of office, the date of the annual meeting, and so on. Information on creating corporate bylaws is also available at most Secretary of State offices and at public libraries.

2. *Revised bylaws for the subsidiaries that recognize the powers of the parent corporation in the governance of the subsidiary.* Linking two or more nonprofits as parent and subsidiary is a comparatively simple matter from the perspective of bylaws alteration. The linkage hinges primarily on the concept of membership in the corporation of the intended subsidiary. Nonprofits have a long history of being membership-based organizations. Some organizations have corporate memberships that are discreet bodies of individuals who actually pay dues and hold meetings and elect the Board of Directors. Newer models designate the current members of the Board of Directors as the corporate members.

When creating a subsidiary-parent relationship, the bylaws section describing individual membership is generally left as it was (though some organizations may want to take this opportunity to update it), with one exception: A new class of member is inserted, called the "Sole Corporate Member."

Alteration to the membership section of the bylaws looks like this:

Article II. Members

Membership of the corporation shall consist of the elected members of its Board of Directors [or whatever the paragraph originally specified] *and [Name given to parent] (the Sole Corporate Member).*

As a result of thorough discussion, the Sole Corporate Member is then assigned certain powers and the subsidiary is also given certain powers. In further sections of the bylaws these powers are individually delineated. For example:

Article IV. Board of Directors

Section 1. General Powers. The affairs of the corporation shall be managed by its Board of Directors. *The strategic plan and annual budgets of the corporation shall be adopted by the Board of Directors with joint approval of the Sole Corporate Member.*

Section 2. Number and Tenure. The affairs, property, and business of the corporation shall be managed by a Board of Directors of not less than seven (7) nor more than twenty-five (25) members. All officers of the corporation shall be members of the Board of Directors. A Director is elected to the Board by a majority vote of members of the Board of Directors, *in consultation with the Sole Corporate Member.* Each Director will hold office for a term of two years and may serve no more than three terms, and may be removed with or without cause by the majority vote of the remaining Directors, *after consultation with the Sole Corporate Member.*

3.   *Application for tax exemption if the parent is to be set up as a nonprofit.* The Internal Revenue Service in your state can supply you with the full set of forms needed in applying for tax exemption. There are several categories of tax exemption, and prior to filing, you may wish to consult with an accounting professional or

attorney who is familiar with the range of options. The IRS will expect a three-year budget projection for the new corporation and will require a narrative explaining the mission and services of the proposed organization and how it will support itself. If the explanation and material you submit are not adequate, the IRS will provide you with assistance by asking very specific written questions, which you will have a limited time to answer. It is not unusual for the entire process to take six to nine months.

    4.   *An operating agreement that defines at least the following:*

- Terms and conditions for creation of the agreement
- Distribution of costs of creating the agreement between parent corporation and subsidiary
- Identification of all positions that will be created within the parent
- Designation of the process by which positions within the parent corporation will initially be filled
- Any changes in titles of subsidiary employees
- Name and location of parent corporation offices
- Services to be provided by the parent to the subsidiary and any costs associated with such services
- How profits and losses of parents and affiliates will be handled
- How the flow of funds between parent and affiliate will be managed
- Definition of flow of routine information between parent and affiliate
- Any assumption of specific liabilities of the subsidiary by the parent or declaration of specific areas of nonliability of parent and subsidiaries for one another
- Agreement on standards or applicability of quality assurance and a description of required remedial actions on the part of the subsidiary if found to be noncompliant
- Trust agreements if any endowments, copyrights, or real estate are to be held separate from the parent corporation or from subsidiaries

Associated Expenses

From the list of enabling documents and the complexity of the issues to be determined in them, it should be apparent that creating a parent corporation is a costly undertaking. There will be considerable expense for legal counsel. The amount of negotiation may require a skilled facilitator to orchestrate the discussions. There are often fairly complex financial formulas that need to be created to govern the start-up costs of the parent as well as to distribute fairly any profit from parent corporation or subsidiary activities. The services of a certified public accountant with experience in constructing such formulas and agreements is recommended.

Risk Factors

The creation of a parent umbrella may or may not mean that the corporations included under the umbrella share in the liabilities of the other member corporations. For instance, if the CEO of the parent corporation wrongfully terminates an employee, are the assets of a subsidiary at risk in any subsequent legal action by the employee? The answer will depend on the structure of the agreement and whether or not there has been public disclosure of the nonliability of the subsidiary for the actions of the parent. In addition, every state has specific laws governing the liability of affiliated corporations for each other's actions. These laws should be carefully reviewed prior to structuring the agreement. Other kinds of liability, such as that which may be created by uniform quality assurance and utilization review, can be minimized in the agreement or through insurance coverage.

Tax Exemption

Unless there are one or more for-profit subsidiaries, it is likely that the parent corporation will be eligible for tax-exempt status. If all the subsidiaries are already tax exempt, their combination under a parent corporation is unlikely to affect their individual tax-exempt status. The mixture of for-profit and nonprofit entities within a single parent corporation requires care. Areas of concern include acquisition of assets of the tax-exempt entities by the non–tax-exempt entities, particularly if the tax-exempt entities have been the recipients of exempt financing or bonds that are still outstanding. These issues do not make the mixing of exempt and nonexempt entities impossible, just more difficult. To repeat a familiar warning, do not try a do-it-yourself approach to this question—seek knowledgeable legal counsel.

Antitrust

Whenever more than one organization is brought under common control, the Antitrust Division of the U.S. Department of Justice or the Federal Trade Commission may determine that a merger has occurred. It is critical to have legal counsel find out whether the planned parent corporation will be subject to premerger filing and advance review under federal antitrust laws. This may or may not lead to scrutiny by the FTC. The Agencies—as these two federal organizations are more commonly known—are concerned when the participants in a parent corporation are direct competitors and the number of providers within a market is relatively small. The creation of the parent corporation would then give a single entity significant control over the services offered in a region.

Labor Relations

As with issues of liability, the degree of integration and control by the parent will determine risk level for labor issues. The likelihood of these issues emerging is increased in the event of layoffs, or if one entity is unionized and the others are not.

Examples

A provider of services to the homeless was interested in creating transitional housing for its clients. Land became available within a large state-owned property and a private investor surfaced who was willing to invest capital at a lower-than-market return. The service provider captured the entire venture in a for-profit subsidiary corporation so as to protect its core operations on behalf of the homeless from liability but still allow excess revenue from the subsidiary to pass to the parent.

A large provider of child welfare services sought to strengthen its clinical services by developing a relationship with a smaller mental health agency. Due to licensing and contractual issues, a merger was out of the question. Instead, the larger agency became the parent of the smaller, allowing maximum program integration while still protecting the corporate integrity, licensure, and state contracts of the smaller entity.

A group of arts organizations representing different disciplines but of similar size met for over a year to determine how best to work together and to position their efforts as a contribution to tourism and economic development. As they discussed how to accomplish this, it became apparent that the groups shared many common problems. As a result, they established an overarching parent corporation that assumed most of the management responsibility, combined the best of their Boards, sought funds on their behalf, and actively marketed both the concept of arts activities and their actual programming. The parent corporation also housed a foundation as a separate subsidiary to raise money for the various groups. The groups decided that the strong linkage established through the corporate parent would accomplish what they needed while still allowing each subsidiary group to function independently from an artistic perspective.

Several community-based health service organizations came together in a rural area with their region's primary hospital to create a network under a corporate parent capable of providing a continuum of services that included the hospital's provision of acute care, a community-based hospice organization providing services to the terminally ill, a home health agency providing in-home support services, a visiting nurse service also providing in-home services, a mental health center providing mental health support to the entire system, a nursing home, and a physicians' association. The physicians' association was organized as a Limited Liability Corporation. All the other members were nonprofit organizations.

Management Issues

There are literally hundreds of individual decisions that must be made as you create a parent corporation to serve your nonprofit's needs. Fortunately, it should be feasible to take your time. A two-to-three-year phase-in is not unusual, and, as with management service organizations, unless there is some compelling reason to rush, slow and steady progress is preferable. Other than their complexity, parent corporations also pose some unique management challenges.

Some regulatory agencies view the inclusion of a nonprofit in a parent corporation as a change in ownership. Before you make the new relationship official, carefully assess its impact on applicable Certificates of Need, state licensure or program certifications, other affiliation agreements entered into by subsidiaries, and service contracts. In some states, the attorney general has been very active in oversight in all affiliations of nonprofits. This is an area that legal counsel should assist with as the degree of oversight varies greatly from state to state.

Parent corporations involve many people at many levels. It is a particular challenge to maintain a common vision among all the various levels of Board members and managers. There is a tendency for the parent corporation to become dominant and to pull away from the other Boards in the system. Interlocking appointments can help, but ongoing and consistent effort needs to be invested in bringing the leadership of the subsidiaries and the parent Board together periodically.

Another difficult area is that of evaluation and problem solving during the phase-in and in the early stages of full implementation. There will be a great deal of activity, of people shifting around in the system. The parent CEO and Board are generally charged with the oversight responsibility for building the system. Setting benchmarks for implementation, determining indicators that will show evidence of success, defining what you want success to be—all these steps can help. A systematic approach to communicating how the effort is doing will also be helpful. This systematic approach needs to be two-way—not just top-down—so that those responsible for system building will hear about problem areas early.

As previously mentioned, there will probably be lots of people shifting within the system. Management is especially likely to shift as the staffing of the corporate parent becomes clear. A key decision for the parent Board is the choice of CEO. Often, a CEO of one of the subsidiaries is chosen, a choice that has its own set of dynamics as someone who was an equal colleague becomes one-up in the hierarchy. There is a real temptation to reward everyone staying in the system with some kind of promotion or title change. (Vice presidents seem to proliferate in the early stages.) However, caution is required here. Parent corporation Board members must beware of stripping the subsidiaries of management strength in the effort to build strong central staffing. The transition will be complex and for each subsidiary the transition will require strength at the helm.

A tactic that may be helpful is the use of a consultancy model. There may be a wealth of talent in the system. Rather than transferring talented individuals to the parent, it may be wiser to arrange for these individuals to act as consultants to their sister and brother organizations within the system.

A particularly sticky area for decision makers is planning for the eventuality of one of the subsidiaries getting into financial trouble. In the early stages, the alliance may or may not have significant cash reserves. Some alliances strictly forbid the transfer of assets between subsidiaries; others set up a cash reserve pool that any member can borrow from (usually at interest). There are a set of complex decisions around the wisdom of creating a consolidated balance sheet and joint borrowing capacity that must be thought through carefully with the help of qualified financial advisers. Some alliances have pulled together a financial advisory group that combines the best talent in the system among managers and Board members to figure out the financial interactions within the system. This is a model that seems to work well. Exhibit 5.1 provides an extensive worksheet for the key power-sharing decisions you will probably encounter as you set up a parent corporation.

Next Chapter

In Chapter Six we will explore the consolidation model that requires the deepest integration of all: mergers. While mergers do not suit every situation, they offer what we think of most often as the primary purpose of consolidating organizations: maximum efficiency. Through mergers, overhead can be reduced or spread over a larger base of programs and duplicative programming can be collapsed. The merger model is the primary means by which smaller, at-risk organizations can salvage important programs that might otherwise disappear.

Exhibit 5.1. Discussion Tool for Allocation of Power Between Parent and Subsidiary.

Allocating Governance and Management Responsibilities

The outline that follows will help you decide how to allocate responsibilities between parent and subsidiary. As you work, bear in mind that there is no one right answer as to how these responsibilities should be allocated—any of the options listed for each decision point can be made to work effectively. The model allows for an even balance of power, or for one that favors either the subsidiary or the parent.

1. Control over the content of and changes to the subsidiary's Articles of Association or sections thereof
   a. The parent Board can alter unilaterally.
   b. The subsidiary Board can alter unilaterally.
   c. Both parent and subsidiary Boards must agree to any alteration.
2. Control over the content of or changes to the parent corporation's Articles of Association or sections thereof
   a. The parent Board can alter unilaterally.
   b. The subsidiary Board can alter unilaterally.
   c. Both parent and subsidiary Boards must agree to any alteration.
3. Control over the content of or changes to the subsidiary's bylaws or sections thereof
   a. The parent Board can alter unilaterally.
   b. The subsidiary Board can alter unilaterally.
   c. Both parent and subsidiary Boards must agree to any alteration.
4. Control over the content of or changes to the parent's bylaws or sections thereof
   a. The parent Board can alter unilaterally.
   b. The subsidiary Board can alter unilaterally.
   c. Both parent and subsidiary Boards must agree to any alteration.
5. Selection of the subsidiary's Board of Directors
   a. The parent Board will choose candidates for and appoint subsidiary Board.
   b. The subsidiary Board will identify its own candidate list, from which the parent Board will choose.

    c. The subsidiary Board will identify its own candidates. The parent Board may advise against any candidate that is not to its liking. The subsidiary Board will take into consideration the opinion of the parent Board but will exercise independent judgment in selecting Board members.

    d. The subsidiary Board will identify its own candidates and elect its own Board.

6. Removal of the subsidiary's Board members

    a. The parent Board may remove members of the subsidiary's Board without cause.

    b. The parent Board may advise the subsidiary Board to remove a member or members.

    c. The subsidiary Board will have the sole power to remove members of its Board.

7. Selection of the parent's Board of Directors

    a. Parent Board will choose candidates for and appoint the parent Board.

    b. The parent Board will identify its own candidates. The subsidiary Board may advise against any candidate that is not to its liking. The parent Board will take into consideration the opinion of the subsidiary Board but will exercise independent judgment in selecting Board members.

    c. The subsidiary Board will identify its own candidates for its own representatives (specific number of seats to be determined) from which the parent Board will choose.

    d. The subsidiary Board will identify its own candidates for its own representatives to the parent Board and will elect them to the parent Board without regard to the opinions of the parent Board.

8. Removal of the parent's Board members

    a. The parent Board may remove members of the parent's Board without cause.

    b. The subsidiary Board may advise the parent Board to remove any member or members.

    c. The subsidiary Board may advise the parent Board to remove any of its own representatives to the parent Board.

    d. The subsidiary Board will have the sole power to remove any of its own representatives to the parent Board.

Exhibit 5.1. (*Continued*)

9. Interlocking membership
   a. The parent will have a set number of seats on the subsidiary Board. The subsidiary will have an equal number of seats on the parent Board.
   b. The parent will have a set number of seats on the subsidiary Board. The subsidiary will have no seats on the parent Board.
   c. The parent will have no seats on the subsidiary Board. The subsidiary will have a set number of seats on the parent Board.
10. Appointment power of the subsidiary's CEO
    a. The CEO of the parent will appoint the CEO of the subsidiary.
    b. The CEO of the parent will appoint the CEO of the subsidiary from three final candidates identified by the subsidiary Board.
    c. The CEO of the parent will conduct the search and present three final candidates to the subsidiary Board for final choice.
    d. The CEO of the parent will provide advice and counsel to the subsidiary Board but the subsidiary Board will undertake its own search and hire its own CEO.
    e. The subsidiary Board will hire its own CEO.
11. Supervision and evaluation of the subsidiary's CEO
    a. The CEO of the parent will supervise and evaluate the CEO of the subsidiary.
    b. The CEO of the parent and the subsidiary Board will jointly supervise and evaluate the CEO of the subsidiary.
    c. The CEO of the parent will provide advice and counsel to the subsidiary Board but the subsidiary Board will supervise and evaluate its own CEO.
    d. The subsidiary Board will supervise and evaluate its own CEO.
12. Removal of the subsidiary's CEO
    a. The CEO of the parent has the sole power to remove the CEO of the subsidiary.
    b. The CEO of the parent and the subsidiary Board will jointly determine the removal of the CEO of the subsidiary.
    c. The subsidiary Board will provide advice and counsel to the CEO of the parent but the CEO of the parent may remove the CEO of the subsidiary.
    d. The CEO of the parent will provide advice and counsel to the subsidiary Board but the subsidiary Board will remove its own CEO.
    e. The subsidiary Board has the sole power to remove its own CEO.

13. Appointment of the parent's CEO

    a. The parent Board will appoint the CEO of the parent.

    b. The parent Board will consult with the subsidiary Board concerning its choice of candidates for CEO of the parent.

    c. The subsidiary Board may veto the candidacy of the parent CEO.

14. Supervision and evaluation of the parent's CEO

    a. The parent Board will have the sole power to supervise and evaluate the parent CEO.

    b. The parent Board will seek input from the subsidiary Board in its supervision and evaluation of the parent CEO.

15. Removal of the parent's CEO

    a. The parent Board will have the sole power to remove the parent corporation's CEO.

    b. The parent Board will consult with the subsidiary Board in its removal of the parent corporation's CEO.

    c. The subsidiary Board may initiate the process of removal of the parent's CEO.

16. Control over naming of the subsidiary and use of its name and logo

    a. The parent Board will have the sole power to name the subsidiary and to determine when and how the name and logo will be used and portrayed.

    b. The parent and subsidiary Boards will jointly determine the subsidiary name and when and how the name and logo will be used and portrayed.

    c. The subsidiary Board will have the sole power over its name and logo and when and how they will be used and portrayed.

17. Financial and programmatic reporting between parent and subsidiary

    a. The parent Board will determine the information that the subsidiary will be required to submit and will determine the information it will provide to the subsidiary.

    b. The parent and subsidiary Boards will jointly determine the information exchange.

    c. The subsidiary Board will determine the financial and programmatic reporting to the parent.

18. Strategic planning for the parent corporation

    a. The parent Board will carry out its own strategic planning.

    b. The parent Board will include representatives from the subsidiary in its planning process.

Exhibit 5.1. (*Continued*)

c. The CEO of the subsidiary will participate in the strategic planning process for the parent.

19. Strategic planning for the subsidiary

   a. The parent Board will determine the strategic direction of the subsidiary.

   b. The subsidiary Board will frame its own strategic intent but will seek approval from the parent Board.

   c. The subsidiary Board will determine its own strategic direction.

20. Control over annual operating budgets and capital budgets

   a. The parent Board will determine all budgets for the subsidiary.

   b. The subsidiary Board will frame its own budgets but will seek approval from the parent Board.

   c. The subsidiary Board will determine its own budgets.

21. Control over the endowments, trusts, and real estate belonging to the subsidiary

   a. All endowments, trusts, and real estate belonging to the subsidiary but not protected by covenant will become the property of the parent corporation under the complete control of the parent Board.

   b. All endowments, trusts, and real estate belonging to the subsidiary will be retained by the subsidiary under the complete control of its Board.

   c. Control over endowments, trusts, and real estate will be divided between the parent corporation and the subsidiary according to an agreed-upon plan.

22. Control over the subsidiary's ability to buy and sell assets

   a. The subsidiary must seek approval from the parent to buy or sell assets with a worth exceeding [$5,000 or some other ceiling].

   b. The subsidiary has sole control over buying and selling its assets.

23. Control over the subsidiary's ability to declare bankruptcy

   a. The subsidiary cannot declare bankruptcy without the agreement of the parent.

   b. The subsidiary can declare bankruptcy independently.

24. Control over the subsidiary's ability to incur debt

    a. The subsidiary must seek approval from the parent to incur debt exceeding [$5,000 or some other ceiling].

    b. The subsidiary can incur debt independently.

25. Control over the subsidiary's ability to sign contracts, leases, and similar documents

    a. The subsidiary must seek approval from the parent to sign any contract or lease that obligates the organization for a sum exceeding [$5,000] annually.

    b. The subsidiary may sign contracts and leases independently.

26. Control over the ability of the subsidiary to enter into cooperative agreements with other organizations

    a. The subsidiary must seek approval from the parent for all cooperative agreements.

    b. The subsidiary must seek approval from the parent for any cooperative agreement that commits organizational resources to a sum exceeding [$5,000].

    c. The subsidiary may independently enter into cooperative agreements.

27. Control over the ability of the subsidiary to enter into other corporate affiliations, including joint ventures

    a. The subsidiary must seek approval from the parent for all corporate affiliations, joint ventures, and so on.

    b. The subsidiary must seek approval from the parent for any corporate affiliation or joint venture agreement that commits organizational resources to a sum exceeding [$5,000].

    c. The subsidiary may independently enter into any corporate affiliation or joint venture.

28. Ownership and copyright for materials created by the subsidiary

    a. The parent corporation will hold ownership and copyright for any materials created by the subsidiary.

    b. The parent and subsidiary will jointly hold ownership and copyright for any materials created by the subsidiary.

    c. The subsidiary will have sole ownership and copyright for any materials it creates.

| **Mergers**

A true *merger* takes place when two corporations combine so thoroughly that neither of the participants survives legally. What emerges is an entirely new entity, with a new name, structure, line of products and services, culture, and so on. The word can also apply to the situation—perhaps more common in the nonprofit sector to date—where two organizations come together and one is absorbed into the other, a process sometimes called *consolidation* and (in the for-profit sector) sometimes called *acquisition*. One corporation legally disappears and the other remains, clearly made larger.

One reason that consolidation has been more common than outright merger in the nonprofit sector is the cost savings to be gained by using all the current enabling documents of one of the entities rather than creating new ones. The other reason for the prevalence of the practice is that, particularly of late, small organizations are most at risk and large ones most capable of absorbing them. In these cases, it is generally the larger organization's name, structure, and culture that inform the consolidated entity. Figure 6.1 sketches the two approaches to mergers.

Best Use

In the for-profit sector, either type of pattern can fall into any of four broad categories, each accomplishing something different. It remains to be seen whether all the standard patterns of mergers will eventually find a place in the nonprofit sector. This section discusses the implications of each of the four categories.

Figure 6.1. Two Types of Merger Activity.

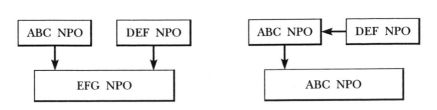

Horizontal

When similar organizations in the same industry come together—say, two hospices or two substance abuse organizations—it is called a *horizontal* merger. Economies of scale in overhead such as administrative or facility costs can result. Expanded production and distribution of services and the extension of effective programs may also occur. The elimination of excess capacity in the market by reducing duplicate services will leave the surviving organization with more market power. All of these may be positive results of horizontal mergers.

Vertical

When two organizations from successive processes in the same industry come together—say, a hospital and a nursing home, a hospital and home care agency, or an infant and toddler center and a preschool—you have a *vertical* merger. The strategy behind this pattern is to increase an organization's influence over consumer choices. For instance, if your child is enrolled in an infant and toddler program and the organization that runs this program opens a day care center for three-to-five-year-olds, it is highly likely, if you are satisfied with the infant and toddler service, that you will seriously consider enrolling your child in the new program. A similar strategy lies behind nursing homes who merge with home care organizations. By providing home care, the nursing home acquires a close relationship with its future consumers. When the time comes for an elderly person to seek residential care, a trusting relationship already exists and the nursing home has probably taken every opportunity to educate the elderly consumer and the consumer's family about its nursing facility. In the nonprofit sector, to date, this vertical consolidation has occurred more often using the parent corporation model.

Conglomerate

When the two organizations are in unrelated fields—say, one that runs a set of group homes for the adult developmentally disabled and a school for behaviorally disordered children, and another that runs a day care center for the general population of children—they form a *conglomerate*. This model allows the resulting organization to diversify its services and its sources of revenue while creating economies of scale at the management level. This approach is probably the least common to date in the nonprofit sector.

Concentric

When the two organizations are in a related field or similar industry but would not (traditionally) be seen as direct competitors—say, a mental health organization and a substance abuse agency, or a mental health agency and a community action agency—it is called a *concentric* merger. As with vertical mergers, this pattern can lead to greater influence over or service to consumers. The consumer target here is those who have multiple needs that span the range of services previously offered by the separate entities. By offering a package of services in one place (one-stop shopping) the merged organization may compete more effectively for consumers on both fronts and provide higher-quality services to consumers with multiple needs. This kind of multidisciplinary merger can also lead to interesting synergy in new product and service development.

Authority and Control

Authority and control structures in a nonprofit organization that is the result of a merger are identical to those in a single nonprofit organization. A single policymaking governing Board oversees a chief executive officer. The difference between a merger of equal organizations and one in which a smaller organization is absorbed by a larger mainly involves how the single resulting governance structure is designed and by whom. If the merger is between genuinely comparable organizations—or if the parties desire to *behave* as if they are comparable—the new corporate structure will be designed by a group of individuals equally representing both the merging entities. In practice, it is often wisest for the acquiring organization to act as though its partner were an equal even if this is not the case and to conduct the process of consolidation with great sensitivity and care.

At issue is who from the prior organizations will have power and control in the new organization. It may be helpful to contrast mergers and the creation of parent corporations to understand the dynamics of the merger design process. The parent corporation model allows for a careful balancing of power among the members and a precise definition of how power will be shared. This balance, once agreed to, is then embedded in organizational structure and is maintained by that structure into the future. Thus if each member organization may appoint three members of the parent corporation Board at first, that right will be protected in the bylaws and five years from now each member will still appoint three members of the parent corporation Board.

This is not the case in a merger. Here, the goal is to create a single organization. To function well following the merger, leadership must integrate two previously separate organizations into one. It is neither possible nor desirable to divide the power in the new organization between representatives of the two previous organizations. While Board seats can be shared initially, all the Board members must have allegiance to the entire new organization and must relinquish their allegiance to their previous organizations. There will be only one CEO. Where parallel positions occurred at other levels in the two organizations, one will be eliminated or made subservient to the other.

Working through the relative power issues to make sure that leadership can take a unified stance toward the new entity can be difficult, but it is well worth the effort. Negotiations should be principled and pay careful attention to respect and fairness. Concern for—and specific efforts to assist—people who will be disadvantaged by the merger also helps. Patterns of victimization that appear in the early stages can haunt the merged entity far into the future.

Alignment of Mission, Values, and Culture

There is ample evidence that a significant reason mergers fail is the inability of the two organizations to integrate at a cultural level. When two organizations become one, their cultures must also become one. In the case of a merger of equals, a new culture must be born of the previous two and everyone must adjust. In a merger of a small organization with a much larger one, the individuals in the smaller entity will generally need to learn and adopt the acquiring entity's culture—but the larger entity has to learn what parts of the smaller organization's culture need protection and preservation so that unique service capabilities are not lost.

The full potency of organizational culture can be seen during a merger or acquisition when two divergent cultures are forced to become one. In the cultural collision that occurs during a merger, the shock for organizational members created by living in a different organizational world can disrupt the entire workings of the newly formed firm (Buono, Bowditch, and Lewis, 1983, p. 482).

Necessary Documentation

When a third entity is created from two organizations, the new entity will require the refiling of all documentation: Articles of Association, bylaws, and tax exemption. When one merges into another, documents dissolving one of the corporations must be filed. In either case, contracts and licenses of the dissolving corporation or corporations must be assigned to the new entity.

Also, in either case, the Board of Directors of each corporation must approve a merger plan. Each state has a format for such plans. Once completed, this plan must be filed with the Secretary of State. The state then issues a certificate of merger to the surviving corporation or new entity.

Associated Expenses

It can be very costly to explore a merger possibility and enact it—but a hasty or slipshod merger can be more expensive still. Maximum due diligence (see Chapter Eight for a full discussion of due diligence) should be undertaken to assess the potential liabilities that will be assumed by the new entity. For larger organizations, due diligence requires the support of accountants and attorneys. For smaller organizations, Board members with financial skills and legal knowledge may be sufficient—though refiling of enabling documents, refiling for licenses, and transfers of deeds of property must all be completed with great care. A close-out audit of the merging organizations is also required. This level of care translates into considerable but well-justified expense.

Risk Factors

Prior to signing any written agreements, a careful review of all federal and state regulations concerning contracts and licenses is necessary, owing to the change in corporate ownership and control following a merger. The degree to which regulations require a specific governance model or physical location of services should receive particular attention. The risk of ignoring this review can be serious. In the instance of a recent merger of a community-action agency and a counseling agency, the local community-action agencies entered into litigation to stop the merger because the counseling agency was given fiscal control over the community-action services. This was perceived as a violation of the federal regulation that requires that these services be controlled by a Board composed of one-third consumers. After a year, the case remains unresolved.

Antitrust

Antitrust regulations may also prevent a merger from occurring. The federal agencies that oversee antitrust have the power to intervene and forbid an alliance that controls too large a share of the market. The antitrust potential of a merger or consolidation needs to be determined as early as possible in the process. Securing adequate legal advice is critical, particularly in determining whether or not premerger filing and advance review under federal antitrust laws will be required.

Labor Relations

Another issue that deserves special attention is labor relations, particularly when there is a union bargaining unit present in one or both of the merging entities. For example, if the clerical staff is unionized in one entity, the bargaining unit that represents it will almost automatically have the right to represent the clerical staff in the merged entity. If there is a disparity in compensation, the cost of including all affected staff in the bargaining unit may be significant. Adequate legal counsel is encouraged to review this matter during negotiations, so that there are no surprises.

Joining a For-Profit Corporation

The Board of Directors of a nonprofit is always vested with the right to dispose of the assets of the organization. Usually, in the case of total dissolution, the bylaws (and also the IRS) require transfer of assets to another nonprofit entity. Recently, however, there have been many instances of nonprofits merging with for-profit corporations. This has happened most spectacularly among hospitals, but has also become apparent among nursing homes, home health agencies, and child welfare, substance abuse, and mental health organizations.

Generally, the for-profit corporation is interested in acquiring the licenses, name, and physical plant of the nonprofit. From a purely business perspective, it is much easier to acquire an exist-ing entity than it is to start from scratch. While this sounds fairly simple, it is not.

There are many complex issues that are involved in these trans-actions. Nonprofits are the result of significant investment on the part of donors, foundations, and sometimes government. What is the return to the public for this investment if the assets of the orga-nization are sold? The law requires that proceeds from any such transaction must remain "in the charitable stream." Proceeds must be transferred to another charitable entity or used to establish a foundation with charitable goals equivalent to the mission of the nonprofit organization. Failure to address these concerns might result in direct intervention by your state's attorney general to stop the transaction.

Establishing fair value for the nonprofit's assets should be undertaken by an investment banking firm or other reviewer with no financial interest in the transaction. The cost of this valuation should be the responsibility of the buyer. However, if the nonprofit has provided large amounts of free care, traditional financial analyses may undervalue the worth of the organization's practice. Courts and state attorney generals have already established that a Board of Directors has a duty to explore alternatives and options that might avoid the sale of assets to a for-profit. Unfortunately, there are no accepted standards for what "duty to explore alternatives and options" means.

Your state attorney general will probably be the best source of information on how a Board may proceed to negotiate and consummate such a sale. Many attorneys general have become very active in monitoring and reviewing such transactions. Prior to entering into any preliminary agreements with a potential buyer, it is wise to consult your state's attorney general to gain the latest perspective on the protocols and process that must be followed.

Loss of Productivity and Market Position

There is considerable ongoing debate in the business world as to whether or not mergers are worthwhile strategic decisions. Business writers point out that if you examine merger history over time, there is "strong evidence that mergers and acquisitions, at least over the past 35 years or so, have hurt more than helped companies and shareholders" (Zweig, 1995, p. 123). While inadequate attention to due diligence by the acquirer or merger partner or unrealistic expectations of possible synergy are cited as common reasons for failures, most often "people problems" are the driving force behind failure.

A factor that clearly contributes to these problems is leadership's failure to anticipate how individuals within the organization will experience the merger process. Certain feelings and behaviors are quite predictable and can be categorized by stage. Exhibit 6.1 lists the stages and attendant effects that were identified by a group of employees whose organizations recently merged.

The ability to predict this pattern should give management some ability to ameliorate the worst effects and to get to what the exhibit refers to as Stage III as quickly as possible. Careful attention to cultural integration and a well-thought-out transition plan

Exhibit 6.1. People and Mergers—
How Problems Develop and Wane.

Premerger
Rampant rumors
Much fear and confusion
Anger that employees have not been consulted
Lack of knowledge of what's going to happen
Not a lot of factual checking out
Drop in productivity
Increase in absenteeism
Extensive copier use for résumé production
People feel excessively vulnerable
Management credibility is questioned

Initiation: Once the Merger Is Confirmed
Personal safety issues arise—"Will I have a job?"
Concerns about changes in duties and job descriptions
Concerns about the future location of the office
Concerns about who new supervisors will be
Concerns about existing workplace rules
Strategies for personal gain develop as individuals try to position
    themselves
Competition among individuals increases
Personal isolation increases
Trust (or the lack of trust) in management will be most apparent now

Stage I of Implementation
The reality of dislocation hits
Some people refuse to cooperate
Fear still apparent
Some benefit to some employees may be evident
Posturing to increase individual visibility
Helplessness of line staff
Communication is limited
Easy to get out of the loop
Trust of supervision and management is low
New learning required
New work groups
Us-versus-them patterns can develop now as the winners and losers
    become apparent

Stage II of Implementation
Frustration with new procedures

Comfort level is rising for some
Need for acquisition of new learning will cause productivity to drop
 for some

Stage III of Implementation
New culture emerges
Incremental adjustment in systems
Clear responsibilities
Settled down
Winners have a new career path
Disaffection of some
Increase in turnover as losers move on

---

can help—see Chapters Ten and Eleven for more detail on these points.

Examples

A family service agency and a children's program merged about three years ago. Culturally, the two agencies were very similar, with identical geographic areas served and similar missions, values, and service profiles. The hopes of the two Boards were fulfilled in the creation of a larger entity with accompanying savings due to economies of scale. More recently, however, the new entity merged again with a more rural family service agency in another part of the state. This merger is far more problematic due to the strong cultural differences, geographic differences, and differences in client profiles and needs.

 A small and struggling substance abuse agency sought a merger partner, identifying several possible alternatives and methodically interviewing the leadership of each. They offered the acquiring partner a location in a rural part of the state, an outpatient capability, and several in-school contracts. Seeking only to protect the integrity of their current program base and therefore services to that community, the Board chose a large multistate substance abuse agency as their partner. They were duly acquired and now their programs function as programs of this larger entity. There has been considerable staff turnover but the program base is intact and growing.

Management Issues

"Any merger is doomed if there is no real effort beforehand to see whether the two cultures have anything in common" (Fish, 1994, p. 68). Assessing the potential for culture clash is an effort that begins in the early stages of negotiation. The task of managing the integration is a step-by-step process with work to do at each juncture along the way. It is the task that will need attention as much as two years following the signing of the agreement. If the integration is handled poorly, the effects of the errors will still be identifiable up to five years later. Clearly cultural integration is the most critical management challenge in a merger process.

If the merger is horizontal, combining two organizations in the same field or business, the likelihood of significant staff redundancy increases. If the two organizations operate in the same region, it is even more likely that one of the motivations for the merger will be to reduce the number of staff positions. In other types of mergers, redundancy is likely to emerge at the management level. In any case, dealing with the elimination of positions, the transfer of employees—and potentially with layoffs of significant numbers of staff—is the second most difficult management challenge. If not carried out with sensitivity, this too is an issue that can have negative effects on the productivity and turnover among the staff who remain.

As we move up the pyramid of restructuring options and increase the risk and the cost, transition planning becomes increasingly important and complex. In a merger, there is as much work to managing the transition as has already been accomplished in the negotiating process. The need for careful transition planning also comes at a time when leadership is tired and ready to take a rest from the emotional pitch of the negotiations and the decision process. It also comes at a time when the executive leadership may be in transition. These are all reasons why it is so often done poorly. One solution may be to do more of it prior to actually signing the agreement. If a first draft of a transition plan is appended to the operating agreement, the early steps can be put in place right away.

Next Chapter

Let's remember where we are. In Chapter One we identified our reasons for considering consolidation as an option. In Chapter Two we explored what we need to do to get ready and to undertake a search for partners. One of our points of preparation was to thoroughly understand our options. Chapters Three through Six have helped us do that. We are now ready to find a partner and begin serious negotiations. Chapter Seven covers the early stages of negotiating and will be particularly useful to organizations who do not have a specific partner in mind. (For those who feel ready to rush ahead, Chapter Eight deals with the later, formal stages when the identity of your partner is clear—but negotiating techniques may come in handy at any time. . . .)

Part Three

Negotiating and Implementing Agreements

Conducting Exploratory Negotiations with Possible Partners

Although it may seem like taking the long way around, it is best to conduct negotiations with another organization in two stages—an early informal stage and a later formal stage—rather than trying to put everything on the table at once. The indirect approach allows the potential partners to make decisions jointly and get to know each other in the new context.

Think through the first contact carefully, deciding who in the other organization would be likeliest to help get a favorable response to the idea from others there, and who in your own organization should make the approach. If your project involves the possibility of corporate restructuring (MSO, parent corporation, or merger), a phone call between Board presidents is in order. This is good protocol even when your organization has issued an RFP and another has responded to it.

After the first phone contact, set up an initial meeting with organization representatives. Again, who attends the initial meeting will depend on the circumstances and the consolidation option under consideration.

The first meeting is an opportunity to share information that is not sensitive in nature and to allow the parties to get to know each other or at least to form first impressions. Pay careful attention to the first impressions you are making—they will be as important as any other information you provide. The objective of this meeting is to establish a comfort level between the parties. It is a good idea if your organization's team develops an agreed-upon agenda before the meeting and defines who will take the lead in each part of the discussion. The exchange in the first meeting often takes this form:

1. Introductions.
2. Informal exchanges.
3. Statement of initiating organization's purpose in calling the meeting.
4. Background on initiating organization's strategic intent: how it got to this point, what it is trying to accomplish. May ask responding potential partner about its strategic direction.
5. Initial reaction by responding organization: questions about the proposed opportunity, perhaps basic overview of its own strategic intent.
6. Response to questions by initiating organization.
7. Expression of interest—or lack of interest—by responding organization. (For the purpose of this summary, let us assume a positive response.)
8. Presentation of process issues and tentative plan by initiating organization, including plans for initial exchange of information such as summaries of strategic plans, annual reports, latest audits.
9. Reaction to process plan by responding organization.
10. Agreement on process to further explore the opportunity.
11. Confirmation of next step.

Treat the follow-up to this encounter with equally great care, remembering to send a thank you note for the time invested. As subsequent meetings unfold, your team needs to steer the discussion to determine whether this potential partner meets the baseline criteria you set previously. There is nothing wrong with revealing what you really want early in the discussions. Potential partners will be grateful to know what matters to you since they will have no more wish than you do to prolong the discussions if your partnership is not feasible.

No matter how these initial discussions turn out, it is a good idea to treat your potential partner as a most valued colleague. It is also very important to be clear about who is communicating what during this period. It is unfortunately easy to mislead or offend a potential partner at this stage, especially if your team is made up of both Board and staff members. Within your team, however that is configured, agree on what information is acceptable for release or discussion with potential partners and whose responsibility it is to lead or initiate discussions.

If you have sought contact with more than one potential partner, you may receive more than one positive response. During this exploratory stage it is acceptable to maintain very positive relationships with more than one potential partner. No one knows where these discussions will lead and there is an old saying about such negotiations: "It ain't over till it's over." Until there is a signed agreement that has been approved by both Boards, it is possible—even probable—that discussions may break off short, so it is truly best to avoid placing all eggs in one basket. Take the greatest possible care, however, to avoid revealing information that has been provided by one potential partner to any other potential partner and to maintain clear lines of communication with each.

When dealing with multiple potential partners, this early stage will be quite confusing to your Board members, particularly when not all Board or committee members attend all meetings. It is well worth recording the process of contacts carefully to avoid confusion in the discussions that may follow. It is also possible that contacts with one or more potential partner will be intermittent. If these wavering negotiations turn serious a year or so down the road, this contact record can be invaluable. Exhibit 7.1 illustrates a contact record showing the kind of information that is most helpful to record.

Judging the Readiness of Potential Partners

In these early meetings, your team members will pick up dozens of impressions, and, when they return home, will try to interpret them. These impressions may or may not be accurate but may nevertheless influence whether or not discussions go forward.

In my experience, there are some Board members (and some staff) who, when included on negotiating teams, are often the first individuals to *read the signs,* to draw conclusions about the success of the relationship based on the observed behavior or unspoken

Exhibit 7.1. Contact Tracking Sheet.

Small Theater, Inc. Contact Tracking Sheet   *Last Update 4/8/98*

Prepared by: Michael Picard, ED

Name of organization: Shakespeare Theater

Key Players: Dana Reyes, Artistic Director; Millicent Gomes, President

Most recent contacts:

Date	Nature of contact	Result
2/5/98	Phone call to Dana	Invited her to lunch on 2/12.
2/12/98	Lunch meeting	Discussion with Dana concerning their needs for performing space. Discussed our concept of sharing our space. Dana will discuss concept with her Board and get back to me by 2/20.
2/18/98	Phone call from Dana	Her Board is interested.
2/25/98	Phone call, letter confirmation	Invited Dana and interested Board members to tour our space.
3/1/98	Tour and meeting	Dana and 3 Board members attended tour and dinner meeting. All were eager to talk about possibilities.
3/7/98	Informal meeting of Board leadership	Meeting of Board presidents to talk about possibilities and process for exploring. No commitments at this time.
3/15/98	Dana and Michael lunch meeting	Strategy session for moving Boards forward.
3/25/98	Informal meeting of Board leadership	Agreement on negotiation teams.

messages from members of the other team. For example, poor eye contact may be interpreted as distrust. Team members who are always quiet may be seen as uninterested. If the CEO dominates the team, the Board may seem to lack commitment or to lack knowledge. It is a good idea to discuss the role of personal impressions in your deliberations with your team and to remind each other that these kinds of assumptions need to be checked for accuracy.

While not all of your negative impressions should end discussions (for example, typos in correspondence do not necessarily indicate a general sloppiness in business practice), there are some indicators that do show evidence of a lack of readiness to move forward. You can count on prolonged negotiations—and should recognize the risk of wasting your time—if these indicators are present:

- Open admission that the Board of Directors is divided on whether to proceed
- Stalling, as may be indicated by comments such as "We want to flirt, not get engaged," or open-ended requests for more time to think about it
- The inability of leadership to indicate a strategic intent or direction or to describe how pursuing this opportunity will help *their* organization
- Reluctance to commit financial resources to the negotiating process
- Rotating spokespersons, sending different people to meetings each time
- Spokespersons who are not empowered to commit on any level (even to process decisions) without going back for approval
- Slow responses to requests for information
- Indications that your potential partner is getting negative feedback from one or more of its funding sources about the project

Narrowing Your Options

The flow chart in Figure 7.1 illustrates how a decision process may proceed when an organization seeks to identify a potential partner from scratch. Although the process can take a fair amount of

Figure 7.1. A Sample Process of Engagement.

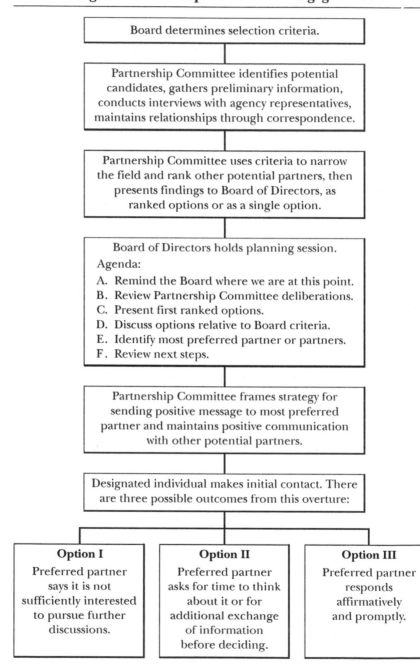

time—six months or more from start to finish is not unusual, and it may be necessary to work your way through more than one list of potential partners or to rethink your baseline criteria if you are unable to locate just what you initially want—it is well worthwhile to give it what it needs. All the background research, the meetings, and the informal discussions help build the competence and confidence of Board members engaging in the process. Talking to several potential partners allows for a full discussion of the advantages and disadvantages of each. And all this processing leads to a Board who will be confident in the final decision. Better a little frustration over apparent delays in the beginning than a lot of second thoughts and recriminations in the end!

Many factors may influence a potential partner's readiness or perceptions of your organization. Its negotiators' perceptions may be mistaken or there may be an individual involved with your organization who may have a poor history with the preferred partner. Also, timing is everything in such matters, and this just may be the wrong moment in this organization's life to consider what you are proposing. Figure 7.2 sketches the possible responses to a negative reply. Variables that may influence the choice between pursuing your first preference and moving on include the degree to which leadership is able to gain insight into the preferred partner's situation and motivation, the existence of viable alternative choices, and the relative patience of your negotiating team. If you can determine the objections and discover that they can be addressed, it may be possible to overcome them. There is a risk here: you may never find out the real reasons and may just waste your time.

If your preferred partner asks for more time to think about the offer—and you have the time to spend—you may try to suggest that that time be used profitably by arranging for further exchanges of information or by hosting a reception for both Boards or key staff. You might suggest that you each create displays about your organizations that could be set up in a reception area or staff room. An exchange of facility tours can also be offered. Figure 7.3 sketches your options in this situation.

If you do get an affirmative and prompt reply to your overtures, it might seem foolish to delay accepting it. However, you do have options, as sketched in Figure 7.4. If this is your first attempt at finding a partner and if you have discovered other attractive potential

Figure 7.2. Potential Responses to Option I.

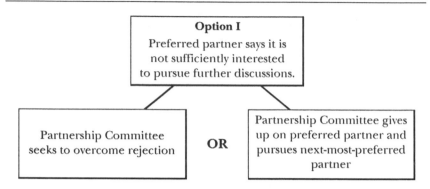

partners in your research, you may want to give them a chance to talk with you as well so that you can generate alternatives for comparison. Issuing an RFP that clearly states your intention of entering into negotiations with another party may spur others to seek you out. Of course, communications with the potential partner you have in hand must be very sensitively handled to ensure that it is not alienated by this move.

Negotiating Style

The members of the negotiating team will bring their own personal styles and history to the table. Their experiences are likely to fall into two distinct patterns: situations they perceived as *win-lose*, where resources were limited and one party could only win at the expense of the other, and situations they perceived as *win-win*, where both parties stood to gain by the negotiation. Some team members may have experience in negotiating only win-lose situations, some may have only win-win experience—and some may have both, or neither.

The kind of negotiating that goes on when consolidation is the issue is for the most part win-win negotiating—that is, it is integrative bargaining, not positional or distributive bargaining. *Integrative bargaining* is "the process of identifying a common, shared, or joint goal and developing a process to achieve it. It is meant to be a collaborative process in which the parties define their 'common problem' and pursue strategies to solve it" (Lewicki and Lit-

Figure 7.3. Potential Responses to Option II.

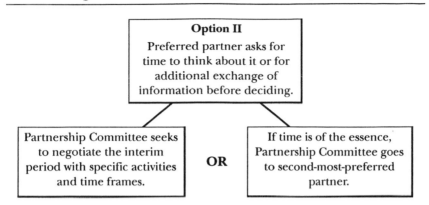

terer, 1985, p. 102). Integrative bargaining is the only choice when you expect to have an ongoing relationship with the other parties. This means that protecting the health of the relationship must be a priority in the negotiation.

In *positional* or *distributive bargaining*, by contrast, the goals of the parties are considered to be mutually exclusive. In these situations, there are only three possible outcomes: "I win and you lose," "I lose and you win," or "We somehow split the resources." This kind of negotiation brings forth typically negative behavior. People engaged in it tend to be aggressive, defensive, manipulative, and scheming. They clearly compete rather than collaborate and often see the other side as the enemy. Winning (getting their way) is everything. How the other party feels when it is over is not important.

The positional bargaining style will not be helpful in negotiating alliances between organizations. To prevent these kinds of positional bargaining behaviors from emerging, the negotiating team leader should openly raise the issue of negotiating style with the team. A useful tool that can be shared with all members is a small paperback called *Getting to Yes* by Roger Fisher and William Ury of the Harvard Negotiation Project (1991). The following summary is drawn from their work.

The first rule of integrative bargaining (or *principled negotiation* as Fisher and Ury call it) is to separate the people from the problem, that is, to be unfailingly polite to, respectful of, and full of concern for the welfare of the people involved in the discussion.

Figure 7.4. Potential Responses to Option III.

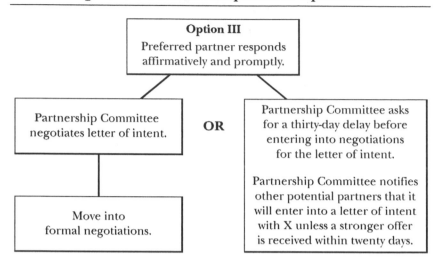

Attack problems vigorously and suggest solutions that are principled and fair and about which you may be passionate—but never, ever attack the other people at the table.

The second basic rule is to focus on interests, not positions. *Interests* are the motives that underlie positions. For instance, one organization may insist that the formula for distribution of profits from a venture be based on annual gross revenues of each partner. The other party may insist with equal vigor that profits are distributed according to a formula based on the relative size of the cash investment in the venture itself. If each party just continues to insist that its solution is most appropriate, the negotiations will go nowhere. Instead, through constructive discussion the two sides can learn to see what is underneath the positions: one party is worried that its size, name, and the prestige that it brings will not be recognized and the other is worried that, as the smaller organization, it will not be treated as an equal. Once the interests are articulated, options to meet these very real concerns can be invented and incorporated into the solution. The solution may not resemble either of the previously held positions.

That example leads to the third rule: look for options for mutual gain. One of the hallmarks of integrative bargaining is the concern for meeting the needs of the party that is opposite you. This means that it is in *your* self-interest for the opposite party to meet *its* needs. When a negotiation meets an obstacle, a place where it appears that the two positions are mutually exclusive, the group moves to brainstorming of options that are not on the table but that each may view as valuable and helpful. The group identifies "objective criteria" with which to judge the worth of the brainstormed ideas. These new and different approaches are then evaluated against the criteria.

This is the fourth rule: use objective criteria to rank options. Objective criteria should be independent of the will of either party but should also be practical to apply. For example, two groups came together to work on competing for major state contracts. Group A felt that an MSO would be sufficient for its needs; Group B thought a parent corporation would be better. Within an hour, the tension in the room rose and Group A was convinced that Group B really wanted a merger and Group B was convinced that Group A wasn't serious about competing for contracts.

The facilitator suggested that they leave the structure decision for the moment and look instead at the components of services that would have to be managed jointly to secure a contract. Over the next several meetings, the representatives thoroughly explored the reality of the business in which they intended to be engaged and developed a list of areas that had to be centrally managed. Once this list was completed, they returned to the structure discussion. They reached agreement on a parent corporation model that included both the capacity to manage a number of systems centrally and the protection of the independent governance of the subsidiaries.

Integrative bargaining is a search process, a search for common ground. If agreement can't be reached right now on the substance of an issue, try to figure out a process to which you can agree that will take you to a different plane or level. Bring in additional information; seek out someone with expertise who can educate everyone in the group. If you can't achieve permanent commitment right now, try for provisional or temporary agreements, the "let's try this out for a few weeks and see how we feel then" approach. If an entire package of proposals is unacceptable, break them down into smaller parts, set aside the ones that are difficult, and get agreements where you can. Then tackle the items that are left.

Next Chapter

Chapter Eight moves on to formal negotiations. It begins with a discussion of the use of outside experts—lawyers, accountants, and consultants or facilitators—to help at this stage. It then deals with the development of the formal context for negotiations: the design of the initial letter of intent or memorandum of understanding.

Negotiating a Formal Agreement

Congratulations! At the close of early stage negotiations, you will have chosen the partner or partners with whom to have substantive discussions. At this point, no organization participating in the discussion has actually committed to the proposed project. Each should, however, be able to state a strong positive inclination to move forward, based on solid knowledge of how the proposed project will serve its own mission.

Outside Experts

One of the first sets of joint decisions that the negotiators will make is whether or not to use the services of a consultant or facilitator, whether or not the group will jointly hire an attorney, and whether or not the services of an accounting professional will be required. This is an important discussion in that these decisions will determine the cost of the formal negotiation process. Given that no organization is yet committed to the project, each organization must understand that the cost of the services constitutes the financial risk attached to exploring the option.

Why Use Outside Experts?

There is only one reason to use outside experts to support formal negotiations: to reduce the feelings of anxiety and uncertainty of the parties to the negotiation. Outside efforts should be focused in those areas where none of the parties has expertise to offer or where objectivity alone will help reduce uncertainty. Let's look at the areas in which outside experts usually operate.

Consultants and facilitators generally provide meeting support to the negotiating teams. They are usually able to assist in both planning and managing the single meetings as well as helping to plan out and manage the sequence of meetings. They can be a resource for team-building activities and can provide important skills and knowledge concerning conflict management. The group must decide whether they want the consultant present at all meetings or just some of them. The roles of the chairperson (often a rotating assignment) and the consultant also need clarification. I consider the consultant to be the quality control on the decision process itself, appropriately concerned with the quality and extent of participation, the pace of discussion and decision making, and the quality of information on which decisions rest. The chairperson works with the consultant to define the agenda and acts as the official host—making introductions, opening the meeting, requesting breaks in the discussion, and closing the meeting. During the discussion, the chairperson supports the agenda by assisting the facilitator in moving the discussion forward, helping with difficult members, and signaling the facilitator for the need to caucus or to slow the discussion for questions.

An attorney is first and foremost the adviser on all aspects of the process with legal implications. In the early stages of discussion, the attorney will research all the pertinent issues relative to licenses, regulatory compliance, tax exemption, Federal Trade Commission rulings, and so on, as well as issues concerning labor law and personnel. Attorneys are also employed to draft (or at least review) the several agreements: from the initial memorandum of understanding to key employee severance agreements to the final operating agreements. In addition, attorneys are often employed to redraft enabling documents: Articles of Association, bylaws, tax exemption filings. When there are significant issues of legal liability or entanglement, attorneys can be involved in *due diligence* (the process of assessing the potential liabilities that will be assumed by the new entity, so that all the participants can enter the relationship with open eyes). I see an additional role of the attorney as solving legal problems or obstacles that may get in the way of accomplishing what the parties want to make happen.

Accounting support is not always necessary. When complex issues concerning financial liabilities surface during due diligence, however, an accounting professional can be helpful in educating the parties as to the seriousness of the concerns raised. Accountants are also very helpful in devising formulas that are equitable in the distribution of revenue and expense in a new venture.

Hiring Outside Experts

Hiring outside experts is not different from hiring employees. An employee without a job description faces an open invitation to problems and misunderstandings, and an outside expert has an equal need for a clearly defined set of tasks. The first step in planning for outside assistance is to agree on the initial set of substantive problems that you want the professional to address. (The list can be amended later in the process if need be.) I suggest that this problem or task list form the basis for competitive proposals so that the group is well aware of the costs that will be incurred.

All the professionals who work with you should share some common attributes. Working on alliance issues is something of a specialty in each of the three fields. One of the special challenges is fairly representing the interests of multiple clients simultaneously without being or appearing to be partisan to the point of view of any one. If possible, your candidates should have previous experience in alliance work. It is also a good idea if they have experience in your industry. If you must choose between alliance work and industry knowledge, however, I would recommend alliance experience. Industry knowledge can be picked up during the process and it is something that you already possess in abundance.

I also suggest that the professionals you choose have experience with nonprofit organizations and that they be well versed in working with Boards of Directors. Professionals who have only worked with for-profit organizations may be strongly inclined to hierarchical, top-down structures and processes. Skills in conflict management and integrative problem solving are a requirement. Beware of professionals who are much better at finding reasons to break deals than make them. Beware also of professionals who do not seem to recognize that the decisions belong to you, the leadership of each organization. They are there to help you solve problems and to make sure that the information on which you make judgments is the best it can be. They are not there to tell you what to do or to make choices for you.

When beginning a relationship with a professional adviser, do not hesitate to request detailed estimates of time, task, and cost before making the decision to hire. Once the adviser has been hired, someone should be given the responsibility to check invoices against the estimate, so that the negotiating committee can have a clear sense of where things stand. If a professional adviser offers a fiat fee to "see you through the process," be sure to ask what activities are covered by the fee. A group of volunteers, without boundaries and parameters, can think up a lot of questions that can be time consuming to answer. In all fairness to your professional adviser, and to your organization's bank account, continuous monitoring of time, task, and expense can avoid serious miscalculations of expense to support these processes.

A further specific caution about hiring an attorney to support a process that involves two or more organizations: Be aware that in choosing a law firm that already represents one or more of the players, it is necessary to sign a "conflict waiver," which, in the event of a dispute arising between the two entities, assigns the right to continued representation to either the new entity or the members. It is a conflict for a law firm to represent both sides in a dispute, and without the conflict waiver, the law firm cannot represent either. The easiest way to deal with this, of course, is to hire an attorney or law firm that has no association with either entity. However, in smaller regions, finding a competent attorney who is not associated with either party may be difficult. In those cases, the aforementioned waiver should be used.

Formal Negotiations

Before working on the actual written agreement that will structure the consolidation, it is helpful to come to agreement on three major areas: first, what it is you are trying to accomplish and the most likely means of accomplishing it; second, the process by which the parties will test each other's fitness for participating in the initiative; and third, the rules that will govern the process of negotiation. All three of these agreements are then captured in a single document that is called a *letter of intent* or *memorandum of understanding.*

Agreeing on Common Purpose and Means

It is best to state what you are trying to accomplish in terms of outcomes. What difference will it make to each party or to the community if this initiative is successful? This should be a careful statement. For example, if your purpose is to create a shared MIS system, describe the capabilities of the system you intend to create. If the system must support outcome evaluation or integrate financial and program data, state this. It should be possible to return to your statement of purpose after a period of time has elapsed and to determine whether or not you have done what you meant to do.

As well, it is important to discuss the range of possible alternatives that you are willing to examine with the other party. There is a very big difference between negotiating a joint venture and negotiating a merger. Clearly, in a merger, the anxiety levels are much higher and there is far more at stake. It is critically important for the parties to agree about what they are setting out to do. In a few cases, the most advantageous structure may not be obvious to the parties at this stage, and yet they feel strongly enough about working on this purpose in concert that they are willing to defer this decision and to make it together as part of their negotiations. While this can work, it is also a risk in that the level of commitment needed to accomplish the intended aims may be more onerous than one of the partners is comfortable with. Deferring this decision is only wise if the relationship between the partners is already well established, healthy, and strong. Even then, it is helpful to outline the menu of possible structural outcomes so that no one is surprised when they come up in discussion. Clearly the concept of merger should be on the table from the beginning if it is, in fact, an option.

It can be a very useful exercise to draft a statement of vision, mission, and values for the initiative with your partner. The joint negotiating team can work together on this and it can then be reviewed by the Boards involved. The process of creating this statement will give the negotiating team something to focus on that is highly positive and that allows everyone to look forward to and define the best that can happen if all goes well. Succeeding at this task always brings a sense of accomplishment and builds a strong conviction that there is common ground here. It also makes it very easy to place the new venture in the context of the mission statements of the partnering organizations and can form the basis of assurance of the individual Boards that this is, in fact, a mission-enhancing endeavor. Exhibit 8.1 presents a sample vision, mission, and values statement.

Testing Each Other's Fitness: The Process of Due Diligence

Due diligence is the process by which each party examines the other to determine its fitness to enter into the proposed agreement. Typically the examination is carried out by an attorney and an accountant hired by each party for this purpose, though Board members with appropriate skills sometimes play this role. The parties agree on the list of documents that will be made available. The document list will vary considerably depending upon the degree to which the consolidation poses risk to the partnering corporations. The more risk, the more thorough the examination should be.

Once the list of documents is agreed upon, the items are transferred to a secure site, a time period is designated, and the examination is carried out. Based on the document review, each party may frame questions for the other. Time is then allowed for explanations to be prepared and provided in writing or at a meeting.

A due diligence examination focuses on determining whether there are fiscal or legal problems that would prevent the partner from keeping the proposed agreement or that would cause financial or legal problems for the new entity. Some potential problem areas include actual or threatened legal action against a partner, unusually high receivables or high levels of uncollectible billings, payments due from government sources that have been challenged by the governmental entity, problems with the IRS, and serious problems identified in an audit or management letter concerning internal controls.

There may be some partners who insist on due diligence prior to signing the letter of intent. This is particularly true in the case of an outright acquisition of assets, and sometimes in the case of mergers. Conducting the due diligence process first gets the issue

Exhibit 8.1. Vision, Mission, and Values Statement.

The Children's Health Network

Vision

We envision a comprehensive service network designed to meet the needs of children and families in our region. The network will provide a complete array of high-quality services capable of assisting children and families in the least restrictive setting.

Mission

Our mission is to consolidate the efforts of a number of diverse organizations currently providing services to children into a single entity that is capable of providing coordinated, comprehensive, and community-based care that is child and family centered.

Guiding Principles

Child welfare services are defined as including, but not limited to, behavioral health, social services, education, juvenile justice, and protective services.

Children who have child welfare needs should have those needs met as close to their home of origin as possible.

Services should be driven by responsiveness to the needs of each child and family.

The network should employ staff who are both bilingual and bicultural in order to ensure that services are culturally diverse and culturally competent.

Consistent standards of care will be maintained throughout the network and services will be outcome driven.

The network is committed to continuous quality improvement.

The primary market for the planned entity will be [geographic region], though the network will also seek additional managed care contracts with private insurers if feasible.

The planned entity will provide single-source contracting, quality assurance, utilization review, joint training, and MIS support to the network members.

of fitness of the partners out of the way and allows the negotiators to move forward with a high degree of mutual confidence.

In other cases, the parties may feel that they do not wish to expend the time and resources on due diligence if they have yet to determine whether they can actually design something together. At the letter of intent stage, the due diligence process is dealt with in one of two ways. Either the precise process is defined—with document lists, site, and time frames—or, when it is not yet clear what kind of entity will be the result of the negotiation, an agreement concerning the process of how due diligence will be defined can be used. For example: *Both parties recognize that a measure of due diligence will be required prior to approval by the Boards of Directors. Since it is not yet known what degree of liability or risk to each agency is involved, the parties agree that an attorney and accountant identified by each organization will meet with the Chief Executive Officers to design the due diligence process. The Boards of Directors agree to abide by the recommendations of this group in the determination of the materials necessary for each party to assess the other.*

Exhibit 8.2 presents a sample list of due diligence documents. This is the type of due diligence list on which a merger or strongly centralized parent corporation might be based. It should be used as a source list for restructuring options in which the parties become liable for one another's legal entanglements and financial liabilities. The parties to the agreement may determine what information is most important to exchange.

Conduct of the Negotiations

As with most human endeavors, it is best to adopt a no-surprises policy in connection with formal negotiations. The prospective partners should agree explicitly on what they will or will not do while the negotiation is in progress. By making—and then keeping—that agreement, they do a great deal to establish and reinforce a sense of mutual trust. In addition to due diligence, the parties need to decide how to handle discussions with other organizations, use of the information developed during their mutual exploration, and competition with each other during and after the process.

It is desirable to develop a list of topics the parties will not discuss with anyone else without each other's permission, generally

Exhibit 8.2. Preliminary Documents for a
Full Due Diligence Process.

A. General corporate records and organization

1. A description of the organization and ownership of the organization, including full disclosure of any organizational or contractual relationships between and among the organization's Board of Directors.

2. A list of jurisdictions in which the organization is qualified to do business or is otherwise operating.

3. The organization's charter documents.

4. A description or organizational chart of the management structure.

5. A list of the officers and directors and biographies or résumés of each.

B. Employees

1. All employment, severance, or similar agreements with any officer, director, or employee.

2. All consulting and management agreements entered into and currently in force.

C. State Licensure and Other Health Care Approvals

1. All state licenses, permits, operating certificates, certificates-of-need, other certificates, accreditation, and approvals for conducting business related to the creation of the new entity.

D. Medicare and Medicaid

1. Any state or federal audit or investigation report relevant to any of the health care operations of the organization.

2. All state and federal survey reports, including statements of deficiencies, plans of correction, and complaint investigations, for each program of the organization.

E. General Business Operation

1. Statistical information concerning the consumer population served by each program operated by the organization, the census data for the previous five years, average length of stay, level of care, and payer mix.

(Continued)

**Exhibit 8.2. Preliminary Documents for a
Full Due Diligence Process.** (*Continued*)

F. Financial Information

1. Financial statements for all completed fiscal years [list past five or other set of years], including the most recent interim period. Such statements should disclose changes in accounting methods from one period to another.

2. Current accounts payable.

3. Current year's budget with accompanying detail.

4. Correspondence with accountants relating to audits for [same period as above], including accountants' letters to management and attorneys' letters delivered in connection with audits.

5. Description of all outstanding indebtedness, including notes, mortgages, and other instruments related thereto.

G. Claims, Litigation, and Arbitration

1. Any letters, correspondence, inquiries, reports, subpoenas, surveys, requests for documents, or any other documents from the [named funding sources, state or federal], any Medicaid fraud unit, state attorney general's office, or any other governmental entity (or private entity acting on behalf of a governmental agency).

2. Identification of any individuals or entities that have been subject to an investigation or enforcement procedure by any of the entities listed in G.1. above and an explanation of the matter and outcome.

3. A summary and status of any ongoing or threatened investigations or claims, adverse actions, litigation or arbitration, or asserted claims against any employee, officer, or director, including reports by loss prevention or a similar entity, for the period [specify years].

4. Description and status of all recent, current, or threatened claims, citations, complaints to regulatory authorities, or proceedings pertaining to alleged failure by the organization to comply with applicable federal, state, or other laws or regulations, including licensure, certificate-of-need, or other permitting laws, environmental and health and safety laws, consumer laws, or employment opportunity laws, and measures presently being taken to ensure compliance.

Please note: Attorneys or accountants may wish to add or subtract from this list.

covering the provision of the planned products or services in specific geographic areas. Parties at this stage often agree to prohibit discussion of any other potential corporate restructuring options until this one is settled. In addition, it is useful to decide what the parties *can* safely discuss with other organizations, such as the collaborative provision of services that are not part of the specific discussions covered by the letter of intent, or ongoing discussions in which one party is currently engaged that are acceptable to the other party.

During the negotiation process and during due diligence, the parties will undoubtedly exchange information that may be *sensitive* (not something they would like to read in the morning papers) or *proprietary* (not something that they would want their competitors to have access to). A formal agreement regarding how such information will be used, both internally and in outside discussions of the negotiations, helps both sides work smoothly and openly with each other. It is particularly useful to be explicit about who the spokespersons on each side will be, and about the timing and content of any announcements.

One risk of entering into negotiations for joint action is that a party working from bad faith may engage in negotiation so as to learn all it can about how to undertake the potential venture, and then, at the expiration of the letter of intent, pursue the venture on its own. To mitigate this risk, it is best to reach a specific agreement that the parties will not enter into any venture competing with the one under discussion. It is often stated that this prohibition will *survive*—that is, that it will last during the period of the letter of intent *and* after its expiration.

Content of the Letter of Intent

A letter of intent or memorandum of understanding captures the substance of the parties' preliminary verbal agreements to proceed with negotiations. The process of developing this document forces the partners to establish specifics on purpose, time frame, and many other matters. These discussions will also clarify what kind of entity is planned and will allow the parties to express concerns and to establish a comfort level around both the content and future structure of the project.

Let's go through the standard content of a letter of intent and briefly analyze why each item is present. Your own attorney may wish to add or subtract content from this standard form and each section should be adjusted to reflect the precise nature of the agreement between the two (or more) parties. To see how this works in practice, look at the sample letter of intent in Appendix D.

Section 1

Orientation to time and participants. For example: *This letter of intent is entered into as of [date] by and between [full corporate names of the parties to the agreement].*

Section 2

A sentence or two describing how the agreement came about and a clear statement of what the negotiation is trying to accomplish. For example:

- *The parties seek to create a parent corporation that will enable the entities to contract as a single entity while maintaining close ties to their local communities.*
- *The parties seek to define how XYZ Corporation will acquire ABC Corporation.*
- *The parties seek to create a joint venture corporation that will be held in common by the parties for the purpose of integrating their case management services for the elderly in the state of [name].*
- *The parties seek to explore a variety of options by which their intended purpose can be accomplished including joint venture agreements, establishment of a parent corporation, and merger.*

Section 3. Purposes

A clear statement of the purposes of the letter of intent. For example: *To define the planning process by which the new entity will be designed and established; to determine targets for completion of various aspects of the process; to govern the conduct of the parties during the planning period.*

Section 4. Expiration

Expiration date of the letter of intent and a statement of how or if the letter of intent can be extended.

Section 5. Agreements Reached to Date

Content of agreements that have already been reached. The following are examples of issues often covered by such early agreements:

- An agreement governing how the expenses of the planning or negotiation process will be divided
- An agreement concerning the information that will be immediately exchanged
- A summary of any main points that have served as the premise of the letter of intent, for example, that the new entity will be jointly owned, or that both parties see the results as a merged organization
- An agreement that each party will devote the necessary human resources to complete the planning process according to the timeline
- The timeline and the major benchmarks
- An agreement that outlines how closure will be accomplished. For example:

    The entire Board of Directors of each organization shall consider the recommendations and shall either accept or reject participation. If the plan is agreed to by both Boards of Directors, then the parties shall enter into a definitive agreement to carry out the terms and conditions of the plan.

Section 6. Conditions of Conduct

This section lists the conditions of conduct during the period covered by the letter of intent. Conditions of conduct are specific behaviors that each party must adhere to. Failure to do so will give the other party just cause to dissolve the agreement. Typically the following areas are covered:

Due Diligence. The agreement of the parties on due diligence issues, as discussed earlier in this chapter, is outlined here.

Discussions with Other Organizations. This section clearly defines what the parties may or may not discuss with other organizations during the period covered by the letter of intent. This section often contains a provision that states that each party must inform the other if approached by any other organization concerning one of the forbidden topics, or that each party must inform the other of any and all collaborative discussions, no matter their content. The section may also define the areas where the parties require each other's approval before proceeding with certain kinds of discussion.

Confidentiality. Letters of intent often contain extensive sections governing confidentiality of the materials exchanged. Specific points covered will usually include at least the following:

- A statement that each party recognizes that failure to adhere to the confidentiality agreements may result in damage to the other party
- An agreement that none of the exchanged materials will be used to the detriment of either party and that all who have access to the materials will be instructed as to their confidential nature
- Instructions as to the process to be followed in case the materials of either party are subpoenaed or either party is asked to give a deposition as to their contents
- An agreement to return all materials without retaining copies, even if an agreement is not reached
- An exemption from liability for any inaccuracies in the exchanged materials
- A statement that exempts information that becomes generally available to the public by another means from these provisions

Internal and Public Announcements. This section covers how internal and external communication about the letter of intent will be handled. It may include the following kinds of statements:

- An agreement that no public statements will be made by any party without the approval of the other
- The specific language that should be used in describing the letter of intent to employees, for example, *"this letter of intent constitutes an exploration of a possible affiliation"*
- The date and timing of an initial press release and the specific process by which it will be prepared and reviewed
- Specific appointment of *sole official spokespersons* for each party for responding to press inquiries

- Agreement that Boards, officers, and employees will refer all press inquiries to the official spokespersons

Noncompetition. This section includes a formal statement that neither party will initiate a venture competing with the potential venture. This section may also include language that defines a process that will be used to settle any potential questions of competing efforts. For example: *If a question arises as to whether a particular set of discussions is, in fact, competitive with this effort, each of the parties agrees that the situation will be discussed in a joint meeting of executive leadership. If one party objects to the discussions, the other party agrees to end the discussions forthwith.*

Section 7. Responsibility
Designation of the individual or individuals who will carry out the responsibilities outlined in the letter of intent.

Section 8. Survival
Specific mention of the sections or paragraphs within the letter of intent that will survive its expiration. The noncompetition clause is often included here.

Section 9. Counterparts
A statement that the letter may be executed in multiple counterparts each of which will be seen as an original, that is, each party will have an identical copy of the agreement, either of which will be viewed as the original agreement.

Section 10. Governing Law
A statement that identifies the state laws under which the letter of intent will be governed and construed. That is, should there be a disagreement that ends up in a court of law, this section designates the state's laws that will be applicable.

Section 11. Signatures and Dates
Letters of intent should be signed by the individual designated by the Board to sign legally binding contracts on behalf of the organization. This may be the Chief Executive Officer or Executive Director or it may be the Board president.

Internal Communication During Formal Negotiations

I will return to the issue of internal and external communication throughout the remaining chapters, but I want to emphasize the importance of careful internal communication here. During formal negotiations, all communication to staff needs to be shaped carefully to send messages of respect and positive regard. Management should openly acknowledge that employees are important stakeholders in the process. During the period covered by the letter of intent, it should be made clear to employees that no firm decision has been reached. The appropriate message is, "We are engaged in the discussion of a possible alliance. We are not yet sure of the outcome and you will be the first to know when we have definitive information." Staff need assurance that they will not read about the outcome in the newspaper nor hear about it from the grapevine. The Golden Rule is a good yardstick for management consideration in planning the internal communication strategy. Controlling the rumor mill is also important. Whenever possible, communication should be face to face—with the opportunity for staff to ask questions—and should be followed by written confirmation.

Next Chapter

With the initial agreement signed, the negotiating team can turn its attention to the design of the new entity. There are two aspects to the design of the consolidated entity: the design of its governance structure and the design of its operations. Chapter Nine explores the issues and process involved in each.

Designing the New Governance Structure

Once the joint negotiating team has chosen a specific model for restructuring, the design of the specific governance structure for the endeavor begins. This chapter describes two approaches to the process of design, each of which is based in a set of values and assumptions about group process. I have used both models successfully and now routinely present them both so that the negotiating team can choose to generate the design with the model that best matches the culture and characteristics of the organizations and individuals involved.

The Incremental, Participative Approach

People and organizations that are most comfortable with this approach tend to share these assumptions and values:

- Groups are more effective when solving problems that can be broken down into discrete pieces.
- Group cohesion can be enhanced by feelings of success in solving problems together.
- A wide-open process that encourages broad-based discussion and that keeps the group from coming to conclusions too quickly will end up taking less time in the end than a closed process that quickly proposes a full-blown concept.
- Building ownership slowly will increase commitment to the outcome.
- When people's anxieties are activated, a clearly structured, step-by-step process can have a reassuring and calming effect.

Let's take a look at each step of the process:

1. *Establish a set of criteria by which to judge the success of the completed design.* Three questions will help the team define the criteria:

What adjectives do we want to be able to use to describe the governance structure when it is complete?

How do we want to feel about the process, discussion, and decisions?

How do we want counterparts to feel about the process, discussion, and decisions?

2. *Establish the ground rules for the process.* Ground rules set up boundaries and parameters for the behavior of group members. The process of setting ground rules allows each individual to suggest "rules" that, if followed, will help to increase the comfort and safety of the members of the group. Further discussion of helpful ground rules can be found later in this chapter.

3. *Develop a complete list of the decisions that must be made in order to complete the governance design.* The length of the list will vary with the structural option that has been chosen. Take care in creating the initial list to think through the issues that are included in a standard approach to the content of operating agreements or bylaws as well as to identify the issues that may be unique to your particular circumstances.

4. *Identify the decisions that members feel may be difficult to reach.* Anyone can nominate any decision as potentially difficult.

5. *Schedule a series of meetings (or one or two longer meetings) to discuss the list from Step 4.* Identify the specific issues that will be discussed at each, placing the decisions that seem more difficult at the end of the series.

6. *For each issue on the table at a meeting, identify the options available.* Discuss the alternatives. Use a formal structure of voting to be sure that general agreement is reached on each issue but consider these nonbinding votes until all the decisions have been made. Keep careful minutes of the meeting and make sure a complete set of minutes is available at each meeting so that the team can go back and check on decisions they have already reached.

7.   *As issues come up and votes are taken, encourage representatives to reality check between meetings via phone conversations with other members of their respective Boards.* If other members of a Board voice strong objections that have not been raised within the team, encourage representatives to bring these concerns back to the group.

8.   *Take the difficult issues that remain and type them up as a survey, with space to write after each one.* Two weeks prior to the time these issues are due to be discussed, distribute the surveys and ask each member of the team to think through the solution that seems best for the new entity. Talk about what "best" means and reach a common definition. Have the surveys returned and collate the responses to determine whether a spontaneous consensus has formed around any of the issues. If so, these issues can be quickly cleared away in the early part of the meeting. For those where the group is still divided, the surveys can be used to generate a list of alternative approaches. Then use these alternatives as the basis for discussion at the meeting.

9.   *Write up the model.* Allow the team members at least a week to review it on their own. Have an attorney review it.

10.   *At the next meeting, examine the strengths and weaknesses in the model as a whole.* Think through various scenarios of problems that might come up and determine whether the model allows appropriate means for resolving these problems. Make any adjustments that are identified as needed by the attorney's review and the group's discussion.

11.   *Write the model up again, if necessary, and then have a final binding vote of the team.* Team members will then bring it back to their own Boards for discussion.

The Centralized Approach

People and organizations that are most comfortable with this approach tend to share these assumptions and values:

- Two or three individuals are more effective in creating a cohesive design than a larger group.
- Most Board members who might serve on a team lack the experience to make good judgments about the issues involved in bringing two organizations together.

- The time of Board volunteers is very scarce, and it will take too long to schedule a series of meetings.
- All parties have a very high trust level in the professionals (CEOs, facilitators, and attorneys) who would be assigned the job of preparing the design.

The centralized approach depends upon an orderly and predictable process. It involves the following steps:

1. *Assigned personnel create the design of the governance structure.* The work group consists of the CEOs (or one Board member from each negotiating team), supported by an attorney or trained facilitator. The design they prepare is fully articulated.

2. *The CEOs distribute the model to their own negotiating team members.* They caucus and identify issues and concerns.

3. *The CEOs meet again and try to resolve any concerns.* (The draft may need to be distributed more than once to resolve all concerns.)

4. *The model is edited and adjusted and distributed to the negotiating team.* Negotiating team members may want to meet in caucus (the members who represent one party to the negotiations) to discuss common concerns prior to sharing the draft with their own Boards. When the proposed model is presented to the full Board, the negotiating team must speak with one voice.

5. *The model is reviewed with the respective Boards.* This is the same process as the one undertaken in Step 7 of the incremental approach.

6. *When both sides have agreed that the model is satisfactory, the full negotiating team meets.* The team formally votes to recommend the model to the respective Boards.

Emotions in the Design Process

Board member feelings and emotions must be seen as important variables in either of these processes. Board members are often as protective of and attached to the status quo of an organization as staff, sometimes more so. This attachment may have arisen because of long service, or because the individual was among the founders, or because the individual is a major donor.

Board member attachment is not the only emotion that is likely to come into play. If we examine the issues and problems that most Board members normally confront, we realize that it is a rare circumstance when Boards are asked to make decisions with significant risk attached. The decisions discussed in this book are of a different magnitude from those involved in passing an annual budget or the CEO's performance review or a change to the personnel policies. Even the adoption of a strategic plan has fail-safes within it . . . if Plan A doesn't work, the Board can go back to the drawing board and adjust. Because of the higher levels of ambiguity and risk that Board members face when contemplating joint action with another organization, feelings of inadequacy may also materialize. Most often, these feelings are never admitted; they show up as behaviors within the negotiating team such as constant complaining, endless objections, or a kind of generalized anger. The danger is that strongly expressed feelings on one side may evoke an equal and opposite reaction on the other.

The most effective means of preventing emotional outbursts is to make the feelings underlying the potential outburst legitimate. It is helpful for each working group to meet as a separate body early in the process so members can talk freely about how they are feeling about the responsibility for negotiating on behalf of their organization. In this smaller and more familiar arena, Board members can ask each other questions or request specific support from their CEO and from each other.

Ground rules are also a useful tool. Fisher and Ury suggest one that is particularly helpful: "Only one person can be angry (or upset) at a time." This ground rule allows group members to let off steam when necessary but also requires other group members to help the individual at that moment rather than reacting to the outburst as a personal affront. A trained facilitator can also assist in defusing tense situations and in structuring the group's process to minimize the likelihood of destructive conflict. Additional useful ground rules that support productive discussion are:

- One voice at a time.
- Listen as an ally.
- Respect diversity of opinion as a strength of the group.
- Heed the suggestions of the facilitator or meeting leader.
- Be brief and to the point.
- When agreeing with other members, it is not necessary to repeat what was said in your own words.

Decisions Concerning the Chief Executive Officer

As noted in Chapter Two (in our discussion of roles and responsibilities in the negotiation process), there are times when the CEOs
of the respective organizations are among those individuals who
will be most seriously affected by the consolidation. This situation
sometimes arises even with the creation of management service
organizations, if the MSO will affect the CEOs' duties or consolidate their jobs into one. It is more likely with the creation of parent corporations, when the existing CEOs of the subsidiaries are
all candidates for the job of CEO of the parent, and a near cer-
tainty in mergers, which always wind up with only one CEO as head
of the new entity. Such negotiations are easiest, of course, when at
least one of the participants has a vacancy in the CEO slot or when
a CEO has already announced plans to retire or move on.

Boards should seriously think about the advantages of consolidation when they face turnover at the CEO level—but consolidation possibilities often arise at other times. Two separate strategies
are needed to address consolidation in an organization whose CEO
would prefer to stay on. Hopefully, carrying out the first strategy
well will eliminate the need for the second.

The first strategy is preventive and concerns the equitable and
fair treatment of the individual currently in a CEO position that
will be affected. As discussed in Chapter Two, the Board of Directors should consider whether a key employee severance agreement
is appropriate. As part of that process, discussions with the CEO
should be held to determine the individual's future career goals,
interest in staying with the organization, and interest in any new
positions that might be created. The key employee severance
agreement will allow the Board to set up a safety net for the individual in case a comparable position cannot be created as part of
the process. Commitments for lump sum severance payments, benefit continuation, job search assistance, references, and help from
individual Board members with introductions can all help to
ensure that the individual CEO has sufficient incentive to maintain a positive attitude toward the process.

A further incentive can be created by the decision concerning
the search for the surviving CEO. The joint negotiating team will
recommend that the search should draw in outside candidates—
or that it should be limited to one of the existing CEOs. It is often

wise both to include external candidates and to treat the existing CEOs with great care and respect within the search process. In this way, the search committee will view all candidates in the context of the range of candidates available. This is a good thing for the long-term health of the new entity, assuring all employees that the best candidate was identified. It also allows each of the existing CEOs the opportunity to participate in the same process and to make a fair case for retention.

Board members must also acknowledge the difficult position of the CEO. If someone has real reservations about the wisdom of moving forward, he or she will naturally tend to make negative comments—and those comments are likely to be viewed as sabotage. In judging a CEO's actions, I believe that care must be taken to assess where and how negative comments are made. If the CEO shares feelings and concerns with the negotiating team, the team should listen carefully to these concerns and take the input as a perspective to consider. That's appropriate. It may even be appropriate for the CEO to present these concerns to the Board as a whole at a regular meeting. If, however, the CEO shares the concerns with other staff or with individual Board members not on the team in an effort to galvanize their support against the initiative, that's trouble.

The preventive strategy outlined in previous paragraphs will discourage undermining but can not guarantee cooperation. It is a fact of life that occasionally, even when treated fairly and with respect, some individuals still choose to attempt to sabotage the process. CEOs at risk are clearly in position to do a great deal of damage in both subtle and obvious ways. As mentioned at the end of Chapter Eight, a communications plan is of critical importance in shaping how employees will view the consolidation. If there is reason to suspect that the CEO cannot be trusted to communicate with staff and other Board members, that role will have to be assumed by the Board president. Again, there is no substitute for face-to-face communication that allows for opportunities to raise and answer questions. These opportunities should always be followed by written confirmation of the known facts to date.

The second strategy comes into play if the first one fails and the situation becomes truly problematic. At this point—unless the CEO makes a convincing case that the consolidation is genuinely a bad idea that should be abandoned—the Board will have to dismiss the

CEO prior to completion of the negotiations. This is a difficult course of action, to say the least, but the Board needs to recognize at the beginning of the process that it is implicit in the original decision to proceed. Everyone engaged in the consolidation process hopes the relationship can be kept constructive, but the separation is easier to deal with if you recognize the possibility in advance than if it comes as a surprise.

Designing Operations

Aside from decision making concerning the CEO, it is inappropriate for Boards to design operations unless the organization is very small. Staff who work in nonprofit organizations are often value-driven individuals who have made the choice to work in this sector because of a serious commitment to a cause or issue. They often have strong professional standards and loyalties as well as well-articulated opinions about the right way to serve consumers. It is always a challenge to lead a group of nonprofit staff members through a process of reconsideration and change, particularly if the planned change implies the need to reconsider current practice. A good rule of thumb for determining participation in planning efforts is to include all individuals who will be affected by the change in the process of planning both the final outcome and the transition to that outcome.

Systemic or Organization-Wide Planning

Systemic or organization-wide planning involves the positioning of the new endeavor within the organization as a whole. For instance, if this is a jointly run pilot project, how will it relate to existing program elements? What should the interactions be? Where are the critical juncture points? If the pilot project is going to run simultaneously in two organizations, how it is treated internally must be consistent. If this is a merger or an acquisition, how will supervisory structures and relationships be affected? What will the organization chart look like? What new programming do you expect to emerge? These are the kinds of questions that must ultimately be answered at the senior management level, though line staff can and should have input into these discussions.

Administrative Support Functions

Administrative support to the new initiative must also be planned. How will the new endeavor affect the personnel function, public relations, accounting, MIS, and fund development? What kind of infrastructure must be built to help make the new entity work? Joint committees of administrative staff are the most effective means of conducting this problem solving. For larger projects, it may be necessary to put together joint staff committees that are more finely broken down, such as an MIS committee that might be given the charge to determine which MIS system will be more effective for tracking results, or a task group on personnel systems charged with identifying all the personnel practices common to the partners as well as flagging those where the differences will become problematic to the management of the endeavor.

Project Planning and Day-to-Day Operations

There may be a time lag in the initiation of planning at the program level. Some organizations choose to delay this level of staff interaction until after the definitive agreement is signed. Reasons for the delay include the desire to protect staff from engaging in time-consuming discussions prior to certain signing of the agreement. In addition, it is at the program level that information about program delivery strategies and quality enhancement efforts is likely to be shared. Some organizations feel the need to protect that information until the alliance agreement is completed.

At the program level, integration should be planned by those who will be held responsible for carrying it out. Day-to-day operations should not be neglected. It is at this level that changes often are most severely tested.

Process Issues in Operations Design

Engaging line staff in a process that anticipates and seeks to prevent problems in the transition will not only save energy later, but will also engage staff in productive activity that increases their ownership and comfort level with the proposed change. As their knowledge of what will occur increases and their sense of being listened to increases, anxiety and stress will decrease. The more quickly rumors and speculation can be replaced with facts, the better.

Anxiety

It is highly likely that anxiety levels will be quite high as the joint staff teams convene. Provide time for staff to get to know one another before attempting joint decision making or problem solving. Team leaders should encourage individuals to talk about how they are feeling—but should also focus the group's attention on the future good that may come from the effort.

Clear Charges and Timelines

When staff teams are formed, the charge to the teams should be very clear, with a written statement of outcomes and timeline. There is nothing more frustrating than working with a group of individuals you don't know well on a task that each individual interprets differently. If there are multiple CEOs involved, they should agree on the precise words that each will use when discussing the team's work. As an example, in setting up an MSO, one CEO discussed the charge to the team with her staff as "exploring the MIS issue in the next few months," while another told her team representatives that she expected "a decision on an MIS system by April 1." It took several confusing meetings in which one staff group eventually accused the other of dragging their feet to figure out why the meeting dynamics were so odd.

Meeting Management

Because there may be high feelings within the staff teams that are quite close to the surface, it is wise to use formal meeting management tools. Minutes should be taken, transcribed, and distributed prior to the next meeting. There should be an agenda for each meeting, with assigned responsibility for tasks. It is helpful to build a broad context for the meeting agendas that lays out the overall process and tasks. Progress should be measured against this overall map or plan.

Leadership

The leadership function within staff teams must be designated by the CEOs. This is a difficult job to assign to an internal staff member. One method of taking the burden off of a single individual is to rotate meeting leadership along with the physical location of meetings. For example, one set of organizations set up a series of staff team meetings. The host site provided the meeting room, the refreshments, the facilitator, and the agenda. Minutes were taken by the staff of the next site in the rotation, who then sent out the minutes and meeting notice and hosted the following meeting.

Use of Decision Criteria

The use of objective decision criteria can also help to defuse underlying emotions. This method suggests that the team think through the criteria that the solution to the problem must satisfy before they attack the problem. For example, if the task is to design an MIS system, what will the system have to accomplish? These criteria can then be used to evaluate the existing systems as well as any new system under consideration. While it may seem strange that anyone would become emotionally attached to an existing MIS system or a package of software to support personnel functions, it is not uncommon for these kinds of decisions to take on the aura of win-lose situations, with an implied and generalized evaluation of the parties as a result. For example, your side is winning because we are going to use your system; you don't have to change, we do; or, your side won on MIS so our side should win on personnel. The use of objective criteria allows for the functional comparison of possible systems against outcomes that have everyone's support. The thinking then becomes: "*Our* new system will be the one that fits *our* future needs best, whether it previously belonged to one of us or not."

Positioning

Even when Boards and CEOs work in a way that emphasizes partnership and equity, these efforts at equity can quickly dissolve when the planning moves to the staff level. The relative size of each organization and the amount of administrative infrastructure can signal inequity from the outset. Consider the case where one organization has one person who serves as both finance and MIS director while another has separate directors for finance and MIS. The director with combined functions will end up on both the finance and MIS teams. This person will do twice the work of either of the other two and may automatically be viewed as "put upon" or "taken advantage of," clearly a position of "one down." Alternatively, the combined director will have a finger in both pies and could be seen as having twice as much influence on the final structure, clearly a position of "one up." Even when there are no structural signals, program staff may search for ways to figure out who is in the top box. While some of this wasted effort is human nature and unavoidable, CEOs must set a clear tone and example for staff and make their intentions relative to "how we want our partners to feel" quite explicit.

Managing Interpersonal Conflicts

When we bring a group of individuals who are new to one another together, they won't all like each other. In fact, personal dislikes can emerge very early among staff teams. Within the staff of one entity, an individual's style of participation may be well accepted and understood. "Oh, that's Frank's way. Yeah, he can be abrupt and abrasive but we know he's harmless. Actually, after you get past all that gruffness, he's a really great guy!" Staff from another organization (already nervous about the transition process) may view this individual's "normal way of interacting" quite differently—and quite negatively. After a few meetings, Frank can become the target for significant hostility. If ignored, these enmities can quickly undermine the productivity of the team. If meeting leadership rotates, the problem is further aggravated in that there is no single individual responsible for maintaining constructive group interaction. Setting an early ground rule for the group can help. The team can agree that anyone who finds the behavior of anyone else irritating as they work together will give the individual feedback privately and allow the individual to alter the behavior. Without such an advance agreement, people tend to avoid talking to each other about problem behavior; they ascribe pernicious intent to each other and suffer in silence, assuming that it's the leader's job to fix things like that—and that the leader's failure to deal with the situation is insensitive or deliberately insulting. "Us and them" becomes entrenched in the form of "We are sensitive and nice to each other, they tolerate nasty people." Most often, there is no pernicious intent and the individual will adjust the behavior if given the chance.

Next Chapter

The culture of an organization is embedded in the images, metaphors, artifacts, beliefs, values, rituals, language, and other symbolic constructs that shape the experience of everyday organizational life. There is no time in an organization's life when culture is more apparent than when it is faced with the prospect of consolidation. Shaping employee experiences so that the merger of cultures takes place constructively is a key variable in creating a successful consolidated entity. These are the topics addressed in Chapter Ten.

Integrating Corporate Cultures

Cultural integration will be an issue to varying degrees as you work with another organization, depending on the option you have chosen to use and the way you are implementing it. Chapters Three through Six introduced the four models—joint ventures and partnerships, management service organizations, parent corporations, and mergers—and gave a brief description of their requirements for cultural alignment. In some cases, it can almost be ignored; in others, cultural integration between or among the partners is necessary to make the consolidation work. In still others, the task becomes the creation of a new culture for the new entity that may bear no resemblance to the culture of the sponsors. Table 10.1 summarizes the cultural requirements of the options, including variations on each.

What Is Culture?

To understand what happens when we try to integrate the cultures of two organizations, we have to understand what culture is and how it works. Corporate culture is generally defined as all the norms of behavior that operate in an organization. These *norms* are made up of the attitudes, customs, values, and beliefs of the individuals in an organization or a unit of an organization, and are expressed by way of the formal and informal work rules that people follow in the workplace. Because organizational units sometimes evolve their own unique culture, organizations with many units may have many cultures in operation.

Table 10.1. Cultural Integration.

Type of Restructuring	Integration	New Culture
Joint ventures that are strictly limited in time and space		
Joint ventures that are integrated into the sponsoring organizations	X	
Joint ventures that are set up as separate from their sponsors		X
Management service organizations within a single sponsor		(for MSO only)
Management service organizations as separate joint venture		X
Parent corporations in which subsidiaries maintain significant autonomy		(for parent)
Parent corporations in which subsidiaries maintain little autonomy	X	(for parent)
Mergers of equals	X	
Mergers of smaller into larger	X	

Origins of Culture

Where do these attitudes, customs, values, and beliefs come from? One theory tells us that culture emerges from the balance that must be struck in every enterprise. When an individual agrees to work for a particular organization, a deal is struck. Individuals trade personal autonomy and freedom to use their time as they see fit in exchange for compensation. Organizations trade compensation for the ability to use individual competencies to achieve organizational ends. The ways in which the trade balances out appear in a dizzying variety across the spectrum of organizations. This variety occurs because the balance is expressed through the manipulation of hundreds of variables. There are so many different approaches that organizations are said to have personalities just as unique as those of each individual employee. That organizational personality is what we call organizational culture.

Gordon Walter talks about culture as the balance between six opposing sets of values that express the balance that is created between the needs of employees for freedom or autonomous action and the needs of the organization to control employee actions (Walter, 1985, pp. 301–310). Figure 10.1 sketches the main elements of this balance.

Security Versus Flexibility

The first of these balanced value sets is a sense of security on the part of employees versus the flexibility that is needed by management to move resources (people) around to create efficiency. In some organizations the rules for moving people around will be captured in union contracts, in others they will be found in personnel policies, and in still others, they will be unwritten or governed by accepted practice. What is fair and right in one organization will not be seen as fair and right in another.

Privacy Versus Scrutiny

Another area of value conflict is in the freedom to determine what tasks will be done when and how to balance work and personal tasks on the part of the employee, and the need to provide scrutiny of the employee to make sure that the employee is doing the work cor-

Figure 10.1. Value Balance.

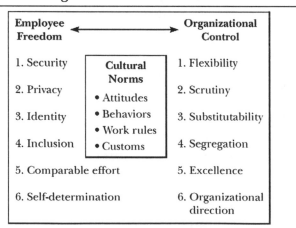

Employee Freedom	Cultural Norms	Organizational Control
1. Security		1. Flexibility
2. Privacy	• Attitudes	2. Scrutiny
3. Identity	• Behaviors	3. Substitutability
	• Work rules	
4. Inclusion	• Customs	4. Segregation
5. Comparable effort		5. Excellence
6. Self-determination		6. Organizational direction

Source: G. A. Walker, "Culture Collisions in Mergers and Acquisitions." In P. J. Frost (Ed.), *Organizational Culture,* copyright © 1985 by Sage Publications. Reprinted by permission of Sage Publications, Inc.

rectly and in sufficient volume. On the official written level this balance will show up in personnel policies concerning performance appraisal but there will also be a volume of unwritten rules about supervision and the rights of employees to manage their own time.

Identity Versus Substitutability

A third area of built-in conflict is the individual's sense of identity that is found at work versus the need of the organization to substitute one person's competence for another's at will. Longevity in individual positions, turnover rates, transfer rates, all tell us a great deal about how this particular balance has been struck in an organization.

Inclusion Versus Segregation

A fourth area of balance is an individual's needs for inclusion and affiliation that are satisfied through work relationships versus the organization's need for achievement. The degree to which organizations do or do not use teams, participative models of planning and management, social events, as well as dress codes, shared vocabulary, and so on are all indicators of whether and how an organization supports the affiliative needs of employees.

Comparable Effort Versus Excellence

The fifth area that must be balanced is the individual's sense of a fair trade-off between compensation for level of effort versus the organization's need for excellence to be competitive. What is good enough effort to continue receiving paychecks in one organization may be either overkill or inadequate in another. As a general rule, organizations need superior performance from employees to survive in a competitive world. How to manipulate all the variables involved in culture to "get excellence" has been the study of a great volume of recent business literature. An interesting aspect of this balancing act is the way that employees help frame the unwritten rules. For example, in many organizations there is an unwritten rule about when to show up for work. The official opening time may be 8:30 A.M., but if you want to make points with the boss, you will be at your desk working at 8:00 A.M. Show up too often at 7:30 and you will hear from coworkers who don't want you to change the yardstick by which commendable effort is measured.

Self-Determination Versus Organizational Direction

The final area of balance is the need of the individual for autonomy and self-actualization versus the organization's need for control to head in a specific direction. An examination of what is
controlled and by whom and at what level will provide indicators
of how an organization defines itself on this continuum. How
much autonomous thinking by individual employees is allowed?
How much of each person's job duties is defined minutely? How
much bureaucracy is in place to control employee actions?

In a recent conversation with a colleague, I was explaining this
model. As the CEO of a very large nonprofit organization, he
responded by asserting that he didn't believe that it works this way.
"I would have thought that I control those things, that it is my job
to determine what the culture of the organization is and should
be." I asked him to think about the times in the last year when he
announced a change in the work rules, and to identify an example
in which he had received negative feedback from employees. I
asked him whether the work rule had changed as a result of the
feedback. He admitted that it had changed. "Oh yeah. I decided
we needed a rule; they helped me figure out how to make the rule
work." While rarely acknowledged in the literature about culture,
the culture of an organization is an informally negotiated agreement between employees and employers.

Given the importance of these issues to employees, it is easy to
see how management action to alter corporate culture by means
of a new alliance can raise employee anxiety to a very high pitch.
What is at risk or at least at issue are all the fundamental principles
that define an individual's work life, including the most basic survival issue—"Will I have a job when this is over?"

Other views of organizational culture add dimensions to the
group of characteristics we have already defined. One of these added
dimensions is the set of variables that determine how the organization chooses to position itself on the values we have discussed. These
variables include history and ownership, size, the technology the
organization employs and the nature of the business activity in which
it is engaged, the nature of the external environment, the pace of
change, and the particular people who are in positions of power and
leadership (Cartwright and Cooper, 1992a, p. 99).

On the other side of the equation, the employee perspective on the value set will be driven by such variables as past management action; trust in the credibility, competence, and wisdom of management and Boards of Directors; the presence of employee unions; longevity; the degree of existing employee cohesion; and, for each individual, the degree to which future well-being seems tied to the future of the organization. (The last item measures relative importance of future attachment, or "How easy will it be for me to get another job?")

Figure 10.2 lays out a simple model of how culture unfolds.

Reactions to Cultural Change

As noted earlier, each employee has struck a bargain with the organization. It is a bargain that is very complex and that is largely unspoken but it allows all the employees to have a sense of security about who they are within the organization, what each can expect to give and to get in return. These exchanges go beyond time and

Figure 10.2. How Culture Unfolds—General Model.

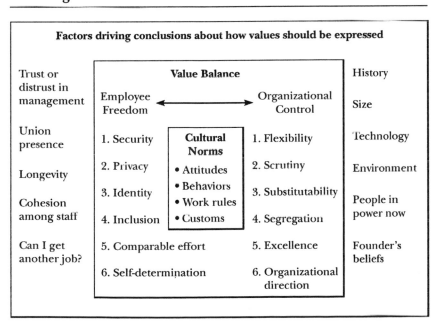

money and include a wide variety of intangibles like membership in a secure group of coworkers, self-esteem, personal and financial security, and the sense of personal competence and contribution.

When a new alliance is rumored or is actually under consideration, each employee must decide whether or not the bargain that he or she has struck will hold if the changes take place. Each must appraise what is likely to happen and to determine whether the future will be enhanced or damaged by this occurrence. Cartwright and Cooper (1996, pp. 49–50) point out the most common merger stresses based upon their extensive research:

- Loss of identity/increased organizational size
- Lack of information/poor or inconsistent communication
- Fear of job loss/demotion
- Career path disrupted
- Possibility of job transfer/location
- Loss or reduction of power, status, and prestige
- Changes in rules, regulations, and procedural and reporting arrangements
- Changes in colleagues, bosses, and subordinates
- Ambiguous reporting systems, roles, and procedures
- Redundancy and devaluation of old skills and expertise
- Personality and culture clashes
- Increased workload

To examine the psychological impact of mergers and acquisitions on the individual, Cartwright and Cooper surveyed a group of 157 middle managers involved in the merger of two United Kingdom building societies. The survey was distributed six months after integration to assess the "degree of cultural compatibility between the merger partners and the extent to which the organizational commitment, job satisfaction, and physical and psychological health of those involved had been effected by the event" (Cartwright and Cooper, 1992b, p. 335). The researchers found the cultures of the two organizations quite compatible and observed that the integration had taken place without significant disruption. However, the survey discovered that the adverse mental health scores of the respondents were significantly higher than the normal population. Noting other negative impacts on employees, they found that "personal survival appears to be equated with the ability to play politics and become noticed [which] may cause individuals to affect or exaggerate extroversion and emphasize to others that they are 'merger-fit.' The continued maintenance of such a pretense is likely to have detrimental consequences" (Cartwright and Cooper, 1992b, p. 343).

Clearly, an individual's self-appraisal in terms of competence, skills, and worth to the organization will influence the appraisal of relative personal risk. Optimism and the ability to see opportunity in change are also personal traits that will sustain an individual in this circumstance.

As the culture of the organization actually begins to change and the individual is forced to redefine the relationship with the employer, the psychological dynamic associated with grief and loss takes over. In a very real sense, the individual employees must lose their former identity (role and relationships) and adopt a new one. Eventually, if an employee remains and is able to discover a new role and set of relationships, the psychological symptoms associated with grief and loss will abate and the new relationship may become more satisfying than the old.

Culture and Nonprofit Organizations

Most of the current literature on consolidation is focused on the experience of for-profit companies. In my experience during the past several years of practice, some aspects of nonprofit management make this picture a bit different, though not dramatically so.

As previously mentioned, nonprofit organizations have large numbers of value-driven staff—individuals who have chosen the work that they do because of very powerful personal value-based choices. I believe that this adds a dimension to both sides of the outermost box of our cultural model. Attachment to mission and to a value set relative to the work itself is a strong driving force for both employees and the individuals who manage and govern nonprofits. It acts to shape both management's perception of what can be asked of employees and employees' perceptions of what is appropriate to give.

Nonprofit organizations include large numbers of nonroutine jobs that are inherently more difficult to supervise and manage and that require a higher degree of individual autonomy to carry out than most jobs in for-profit companies. I believe that the baseline expectations of employees concerning their autonomous actions is higher in many nonprofit organizations.

In addition, there is a high percentage of college-educated professionals, many of whom have strong ties and loyalties to the professional ethics of their field. They measure their self-worth and the worth of their job tasks with an additional yardstick, the degree to which they are true to their profession's standards. Many unflinchingly act as advocates for the perspectives of their profession and these loyalties will be as strong as any sense of organizational affiliation.

Because so many nonprofits deal with intangibles, there are often fewer direct means of measuring performance than in the for-profit world, though with the increase in outcome assessment this is changing. When these objective measures are not present or are not articulated, it muddies the waters around productivity, excellence, and comparable effort.

Most nonprofits also manage two separate systems simultaneously: the system to obtain resources to operate and the system to secure and serve consumers. In a for-profit organization, this is one system. The consumers *purchase* products and services, so revenue generation and service or product delivery are simultaneous. In a nonprofit that survives on foundation grants, donations, and government contracts, how and whether consumers are well served may have little or nothing to do with whether the organization has revenue. On the employer side, we must add the influence of funding sources as a significant environmental driving force.

Nonprofits who use volunteers also manage two compensation systems: one for paid staff and another for volunteers. The tangible part of the psychological contract is absent from the relationship with volunteers, but the intangible elements are often as strong or stronger. As an example, a few years ago I worked with an organization that provided crisis counseling over the phone. This was a very small organization with four paid staff but well over a hundred volunteers. The Board and CEO were convinced that the organization should merge with a larger entity due to its difficulty in securing operating funds. A large group of volunteers organized and brought an alternative to the Board that showed how volunteers could replace half of the paid staff. The agency maintains its independence to this day.

These attributes of nonprofits, then, alter the model slightly, as shown in Figure 10.3.

This said, I do not believe that nonprofit staff experience the threat or actuality of consolidation in a different way from for-profit employees. I have observed the same degree of upset, anxiety, grief, and loss. I do think that bringing some of the differences between nonprofits and for-profits to the surface helps us to understand what kind of action is required on the part of those who must make choices about consolidation partners and who must manage the transition once the final agreement is reached. Before looking more closely at those tasks, let's look at how we can get to know our own culture and that of our potential partners.

Figuring Out Culture Type

Cartwright and Cooper (1996, pp. 57–81) describe four culture types: power cultures, role cultures, task/achievement cultures, and person/support cultures. It is useful to explore these types in some detail.

Figure 10.3. How Culture Unfolds—Nonprofit Model.

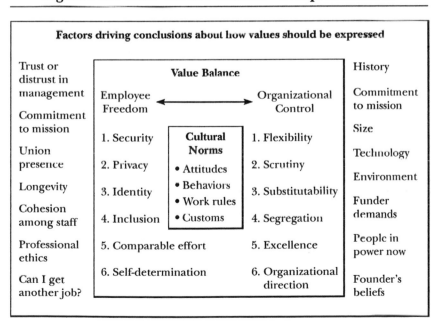

Power Cultures

While this culture profile is not common within the nonprofit sector, it does occur, particularly within organizations that are run by their founders or led by a highly charismatic leader or advocate as CEO. Characteristically, power cultures tend to display these attributes:

- Power is held by a single individual or a very small group.
- Individual rather than group decision making is the norm.
- Decisions tend to be based as much on intuition and past successes as on logical reasoning.
- Individual members are motivated by a sense of personal loyalty to superiors, or by fear of superiors.
- Reward systems are typically inequitable, and more likely to be based on personal preference of superiors than on objective performance criteria.
- Managers are generally autocratic and suppressive of challenge.
- "Employee does what he or she is told."

Role Cultures

In my experience, this profile is likely to emerge in larger, older nonprofits who see themselves as having attained institutional status. It shows the following attributes:

- Guiding principles are logic, rationality, and the achievement of maximum efficiency.
- The organization is viewed as a collection of roles to be undertaken rather than a collection of people and personalities.
- Things get done according to highly structured and articulated procedures. A good employee is one who recognizes protocol and sticks to the rules.
- Power is distributed hierarchically.
- Procedures offer security and predictability to the individual employee but often constrain innovative and risk-taking behavior.
- "Employee acts within the parameters of the job description."

Task/Achievement Cultures

I believe that this is the most common culture profile in the non-profit sector. Do you recognize these attributes from your own experience?

- Emphasis is placed on accomplishing the task. What is achieved is viewed as more important than how it is achieved.
- A team culture is the norm—commitment to the individual task bonds and energizes the individuals.
- Relevant task expertise is highly valued and frequently is seen as more influential than personal or positional power.
- Operations are characterized by flexibility and high levels of worker autonomy.
- When things go wrong, there is a tendency for everyone to blame everyone else.
- "The employee acts in the way he or she considers suitable for the task."

Person/Support Cultures

Among nonprofits, this profile seems to emerge in subunits or programs of larger organizations, particularly within organizations employing groups of highly trained professionals and in arts collaboratives. In the for-profit world, it is typically found among consulting practices, law offices, and subcultures of larger organizations such as Research and Development units. Such organizations tend to show these attributes:

- They tend to be egalitarian. Structure is minimal; the culture exists and functions solely to nurture the personal growth and development of its individual members.
- Information, influence, and decision making are shared collectively.
- "The employee does his or her own thing."

Combined Cultures

We have to remember when thinking about culture type that organizations can also be hybrids. I can think of several previous clients whose employees describe the workplace "like a family." While certainly a task/achievement element is strongly present, the person/support characteristics are also present.

Cartwright and Cooper show us that problems arise when we attempt to combine cultures that ask employees to move from right to left on the diagram in Figure 10.4. Employees who have experienced a fairly high degree of autonomy often resist giving up that autonomy. To a lesser degree, resistance can also arise among employees who must give up the security of a role culture and take on the increased ambiguity of task/achievement—a circumstance that many organizations face as they attempt to bring customer focus to bureaucratic organizations. Debilitating clashes will occur if we attempt to merge a power culture with a person/support or task/achievement culture, particularly if the power culture emerges as dominant.

Predicting Culture Clash

The first step is to determine the nature of your organization's culture and that of your potential partner. Appendix E contains a list of questions that can be used in a focus group format to gain insight from your employees—though CEOs, senior managers, and Boards with whom I have worked have been able to type themselves without difficulty, even identifying specific programs with differing culture types within their organizations.

In the early stages of negotiation, determining your potential partner's culture type may be more difficult. Hints may be found in vision and mission statements that contain values or beliefs. In early discussions, you may gain a sense of how decisions are reached

Figure 10.4. Cultural Spectrum.

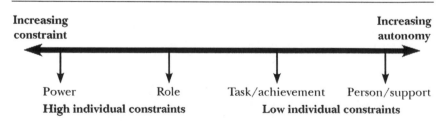

Source: S. Cartwright and C. L. Cooper, *Managing Mergers, Acquisitions, and Strategic Alliances: Integrating People and Cultures.* Oxford, England: Butterworth-Heinemann, 1996, p. 80. Reprinted by permission of the publisher.

within the organization as well as the CEO's style and approach. During tours or visits to potential partner offices, you may also gain a sense of the level of stress in personal interactions—and as your staffs come to know one another, their interactions will indicate a great deal about how your potential partner's culture operates. You will want to listen carefully when people return from joint meetings.

The negotiating style of the potential partner can also be a strong indicator. Does the CEO draw lines in the sand and make nonnegotiable demands? Do negotiators play power games? Do they seem to have a very high need to control the negotiating process? Are they adamant about the need to create a top-down, hierarchical structure for the new entity? If any of these indicators are present, it probably means that this is a power culture. Depending upon where your organization is on the scale, you may decide that the partnership won't work or you may simply recognize that the task of integration will be very difficult and adjust your transition planning to recognize the level of difficulty.

If you have moved into formal negotiation, the topic of culture match can be put on the table as an issue to explore. Both negotiating teams may need some education about why this is an important issue—but exploring it together is preferable to each of you trying to figure it out on your own. All parties must recognize the relationship between the planned endeavor and the need to integrate the culture of the partners or create a new culture suitable for the new entity. One way to compare and contrast the various aspects of how culture is expressed is to use the questions listed in Appendix E with a cross-section of employees from each potential partner. It is best to use a skilled facilitator to conduct these sessions and to collate and feed back the results.

Reducing the Negative Effects of Culture Integration

Leadership has several options when approaching culture change. *Aggressive* efforts tend to define the new cultural expectations quickly and definitively and to offer employees little participation and less choice. *Corrosive* efforts couple aggressive redefinition with threats and punishment for noncompliance. *Facilitative and educational* efforts attempt to involve employees in determining the most appropriate culture for what the organization needs to accomplish, allowing for participation in reinventing behavioral norms and redefining the events, rituals, and artifacts that go with the new culture.

Given the value-driven nature of employees in nonprofit organizations and the preponderance of task/achievement cultures, it is highly likely that the aggressive or corrosive approaches will yield serious morale problems and high turnover. If the new venture depends on the continued employment of key staff and their continuing good will, it is advisable to use facilitation and education as the model for culture change.

Within such a process, the role of leadership is to move employees from their initial anxiety to a state of positive excitement about the potential of the new venture. There are four definable phases to this transition.

- Phase One: Build ownership and excitement over vision, mission, and values of new venture.
- Phase Two: Engage staff in planning the operational transition; define clearly any adjustments in roles.
- Phase Three: Allow employees to participate in choosing the cultural model that they believe will most effectively support the vision, mission, and values of the new venture.
- Phase Four: Allow employees to work in teams to determine how any cultural change will influence what they do and how they behave. Use objective decision criteria routinely within these discussions and keep the outcome in plain sight.

General Recommendations for Culture Integration

I believe that open processes work far better in the nonprofit world than secret processes. As stated earlier, Board members and employees need to be educated about the environment in which the organization operates and what the planned venture will contribute to the mission. The vision for the new venture must be kept in front of everyone all the time. If there is anything that will help staff and Board through a difficult period, it is the absolute conviction that what they are going through will be good for the community, for their consumers, for making the world a better place. Within that overall framework, there are a number of specific measures that will help make things go smoothly.

- *Try not to prolong negotiations over long periods of time.* Recognize that prolonged uncertainty is tough on people; as a general rule, few of us thrive on ambiguity. One of the potent destructive elements in these situations is employees' sense of powerlessness. In creating a new culture or integrating cultures, move quickly with a process to create a new cultural context. The transition can be eased if this is a participative process in which employees and management work together to design the culture that they believe will best serve the interests of the new or combined entity.

- *Allow some experimentation about the new culture.* Decisions can be reached tentatively, then tried out and evaluated. As an evaluation method, you may want to consider a staff liaison system, with an individual identified at each level or within each programmatic unit who will serve as the contact for staff with concerns or feedback.

- *Provide help with stress management.* This can anticipate any change process before it is actually under way. Skill building among managers and training for staff sends the message that you care about the employees and how they react to the situation. Through such a vehicle, employees can learn about the grieving process, why they feel the way they do. In developing a context to understand their feelings and emotions, they gain understanding of where they are.

- *Help employees with personal decision making about staying or going.* If there are to be layoffs or turnover emerges as an issue, allow the remaining employees to talk about it, to vent their feelings and emotions. It is wise as well to allow employees who leave to say good-bye properly even though this may mean a period of multiple farewell events, something that can in and of itself drain energy from everyone.

Next Chapter

In Chapter Eleven we will examine the approval of final agreements and look at issues of communication with external constituents. We will also explore the process of transition planning.

Finalizing Definitive Agreements and Planning the Transition

As the governance and staff teams conclude their planning, the Board team looks over the results and discusses and reviews the proposed plans. All the major agreements that have been reached are then incorporated into a tentative set of final documents.

Each partner to the endeavor should have its own attorney review these materials. The partners then discuss any reservations that emerge at this point, adapting the documents as necessary and mutually agreeable. When there are no further adjustments, the documents as they stand at that point become the definitive agreements. These are the agreements that will be signed and adopted by the respective Boards and that will have the legal standing of contracts between or among the parties.

Once the final set of documents has been prepared, it is customary to hold a joint education session for the full Boards of all the partners. This is most often a two- to three-hour meeting where the content of the definitive agreements is presented and Board and staff team members (often along with their advising attorney and accountant) address any questions and concerns that Board members new to the process may raise. Such questions and concerns should be encouraged rather than discouraged or brushed off—it is entirely possible that a fresh eye may see something that escaped everyone up to this point. If serious concerns surface, the Board team may decide to reconvene following the meeting to deal with the issues in an effort to head off a rejection of the agreements.

Following the timeline set out in the original letter of intent, the Boards will determine a date on which they will meet separately to consider and adopt the agreements. It is customary to make these meetings simultaneous if possible. If not, it is best to schedule them as close together as can be managed. This is particularly important if there are several corporate parties to the agreement. If one of the parties meets and rejects the agreement and others hear about the rejection prior to their own vote, it could negatively bias their consideration.

The one exception to this process may be bylaw changes. If the endeavor requires an adjustment to the partners' bylaws, each organization must follow its own procedures for such changes. In some cases, bylaws can only be amended at an annual meeting specifically designated for a particular month that may be quite distant from planned simultaneous meetings of the Boards. In such a case, the definitive agreements will specify the proposed bylaw change and recognize that the change must occur in compliance with the procedure that governs that particular party.

Once the Boards have voted, the several copies of the agreements are signed and distributed so that each party retains its own full set.

Internal Announcements

Cartwright and Cooper (1996), in their study of mergers and acquisitions, stress the importance of the first announcement that the agreement has been ratified. While their comments focus specifically on acquisitions in which all the negotiations may have occurred in secret, I believe that their caution is equally valid for any announcement involving significant organizational change that affects employees in a nonprofit organization. It certainly fits in with the general recommendations on culture integration.

> Following the acquisition or merger, a new psychological contract between the individual and the organization has to be established. The acquisition announcement is an important first stage in setting the scene for the renegotiation of that contract. Acquiring management should respond by approaching the announcement as an invitation to acquired employees to join the new organization.

The objective of the acquisition announcement should be to achieve a balance between presenting an optimistic view of the future without appearing over critical of past endeavours. It should clearly prepare employees for change, but at the same time demonstrate sensitivity and an awareness of their concerns. If the acquisition announcement is unconvincing, poorly handled or fails to meet these objectives, there is a danger that it will be interpreted as a declaration of war rather than an invitation to cooperate and work together [Cartwright and Cooper, 1996, p. 119].

Managing Relationships with External Constituents

One of the unique aspects of managing a nonprofit organization is the relative power of external constituencies. Funders, other collaborative partners, donors, and consumers can create major impediments for a planned consolidation if communication is not handled well.

Funders

A few funding sources have actually established policies that govern working relationships or mergers among their nonprofit contractors. An obvious first step is to check with all your organization's funders to determine whether any such policies or protocols have been developed. If not, the steps listed here should prevent any concerns or problems with existing funders.

1. *As soon as the letter of intent is signed, contact each funder by phone and announce the start of negotiations.* Gain a sense of the funder's initial reaction to the proposed process or project.

2. *Follow this phone call with written notification.* It is never safe to assume that both parties to a phone conversation came away with the same understanding of what was said.

3. *At the point at which definitive agreements have been reached, contact each funder again by phone and inform it of the progress achieved.* If someone requests a meeting to learn more, schedule it prior to the final vote of the Board of Directors. If a major funder has a major objection that is critical to overcome, your Board of Directors will need to know.

4. *Again, follow up with written confirmation of whatever under-standing you have reached over the phone or in person.* For instance, if the funder has agreed during your conversations that the proposed relationship will not affect any existing grants or contracts, that assurance should be fed back to be sure that you have heard the message correctly.

Other Collaborative Partners

Similarly, you do not want your existing collaborative partners to find out about what you are doing from the newspapers. Care must be taken if you have agreed to keep the negotiations confidential but this should be an issue that is negotiated with your partners. As noted earlier, partners should agree to language that can be used publicly, not only with employees but with other organizations.

Donors

As several hospitals and health care organizations have discovered recently, long-standing donors can be very sensitive to major changes in ownership or control or changes in physical plant or location. This is particularly true of organizations that have been supported by significant charitable gifts. Donors who have given major sums over a long period often have what amounts to a proprietary sense of ownership over the organization.

Such individuals require a special measure of care as the negotiating process unfolds. There is significant deference required in efforts to educate major donors as to the planned change. After all, the new entity may still need their support.

Focus groups or interviews early in the process can help these individuals feel that they have been consulted. These conversations do not necessarily have to be definitive, rather, they can be couched as a series of what-ifs. These occasions can also be used as early efforts to educate donors about the circumstances of the organization. A good interviewer or facilitator can probe for their knowledge of how the environment has changed and can test for whether their perception of the organization is realistic, gently bringing their perceptions into line. Donors often respond well if they are helped to understand how the community or the consumers will be better off. When there is a clearly articulated statement of how the planned consolidation will enhance mission, donors may even be motivated to assist financially with the process.

Consumers

Consumers are another group where special care should be taken in communication. When the planned change is a major one, consumer anxiety should be taken as seriously as employee anxiety. Primary questions from the consumer's perspective: "Will the services I receive change in any way?" "Will the staff I know still be there?" "Will I be able to go to the same place to get my services?"

It is rare that generic public announcements will deal effectively with consumer anxiety. In this instance, there is no substitute for one-on-one communication. As soon as the degree of impact on consumers is known, these facts should be communicated directly, ideally by staff they know. If the volume of consumers prevents this approach, a personal letter is an acceptable substitute. Information educating consumers about the changes (or reassuring them about the lack of change in their services) should be included in organizational newsletters for at least three or four months following implementation.

The Transition Plan

By the time the final agreements are signed, transition planning will have begun. The overall governance structures, choice of leadership, and operational plans are all essential to the transition, and they will be included in the definitive agreements themselves. The communication plan to date is also part of the transition. Beyond these major areas, however, there is much to be done to bring the hoped-for alliance to reality as a successful venture.

A clear priority is to ensure that service quality and quantity do not deteriorate. The most serious threats to service continuity are likely to be plummeting staff morale and unplanned turnover of staff, sometimes considered an inevitable result of consolidation. Turnover will be reduced or at least slowed down by appropriate support of the staff. As noted earlier, severance agreements may have already been negotiated. Skill building in stress management acknowledges the emotional state of employees and sends the message that the people managing the transition care about the employees. Forums to deal with staff questions and concerns should continue to be scheduled through the first year of the transition. Anonymous suggestion boxes in which staff can deposit their concerns may also help. Engagement of staff in the design of day-to-day operations has already been discussed in Chapters Nine and Ten, and it is part of the overall effort to help employees become as comfortable as possible as quickly as possible. Concerted efforts at building constructive relationships among staff who have not worked together previously sometimes include social events as well as work teams.

Guide to Transition Planning Issues

The outline in Exhibit 11.1 can serve as a guide or checklist to ensure that your transition plan has addressed all relevant issues. In each area, a specific strategy with timelines should be articulated. The list covers the areas most likely to be affected by any consolidation, though to different degrees in the different models and variants. You may want to delete some or add others to suit your own organization's situation.

Given the importance of the transition to the success of the new venture, it is worth summarizing and restating the goals for this critical period:

- To protect relationships with consumers by avoiding any major disruptions in service and productivity
- To reduce staff anxiety and promote reassurance and movement through the period of grief and loss
- To reinforce organizational commitment and loyalty to the new venture at the earliest opportunity
- To promote retention of key staff and to eliminate unnecessary turnover
- To adjust management systems to support the new venture
- To provide correct and reliable information throughout the transition and to engender staff support in reducing rumors and misinformation

Exhibit 11.1. Transition Planning Checklist.

___ Changes in programs and services
    ___ Programs expanded
    ___ Programs added
    ___ Programs reduced in size
    ___ Programs eliminated
    ___ Quality assurance
    ___ Service continuity
___ Governance
    ___ Bylaw changes
    ___ Nomination of new Board
    ___ Orientation
___ CEO-level leadership
___ Senior management changes
___ Personnel
    ___ Layoffs
    ___ Additional hires
    ___ Staff transfers
    ___ Labor issues
    ___ Adjustments to salaries and benefits
    ___ Adjustment to personnel policies
___ Finance
    ___ Budget
    ___ Formulas for distribution of revenue and expense
    ___ System for tracking information
    ___ Vendor relationships
___ Legal aspects
    ___ Articles of Association
    ___ Bylaws
    ___ Operating agreements
    ___ Contracts
    ___ Licenses
    ___ Federal Trade Commission filings
    ___ Tax status
___ Marketing
    ___ Name
    ___ Logo
    ___ Signage
    ___ Brochures and other public relations materials

___ Constituent relations
    ___ Consumers
    ___ Funders
    ___ Donors
    ___ Other collaborative partners
    ___ General public
___ Internal communication
    ___ Roles and responsibilities for internal communication
    ___ Staff forums
    ___ Written confirmations
    ___ Staff liaisons
    ___ Suggestion box
___ Staff support
    ___ Stress management
    ___ One-on-one counseling
    ___ Rumor control
___ Culture redesign
    ___ Roles and responsibilities
    ___ Staff participation strategy
    ___ Evaluation and readjustment
___ Physical plant adjustments
___ Method and roles and responsibilities for evaluation of progress of the transition plan

---

- To integrate or bring a new organizational culture into existence
- To evaluate and adjust the culture to the changing needs of the alliance

Next Chapter

Recently, I worked with the Board and staff of a small and struggling agency that serves cancer patients in their efforts to figure out whether or not to look for a partner who could help them sustain what they have built over the last eight years. At the end of a day-long retreat, one of the Board members approached me and said that of everything that had been said that day, she hoped that her fellow Board members would remember what I had said right after lunch. "What was that?" I asked, a bit tired. "You said that we should measure the potential success of any future partnership with one criteria: 'Can it enhance our mission accomplishment? Will it sustain or make our mission come more alive in the world?' You said, 'There isn't any other reason to attempt this.'"

While I have included some closing thoughts in the Epilogue, clearly the next chapter in the nonprofit sector's efforts to consolidate will be written by you—the leadership of nonprofit organizations. As you proceed, it is my hope that you will remember where we began this discussion—viewing consolidation as a tool to serve the purposes and constituencies for which your organization was created.

Epilogue

It seems to me that we live in an era that will surely challenge the learning capacities of each of us and of all the organizations we lead. In the course of working with my clients over the last few years and preparing this material, I have learned a great deal, not only about the content captured in this book but also about people facing significant change and about what we do and don't have choices about.

We must accept, I think, that change of sufficient magnitude can fracture the social contract within an organization. As the base of resources shifts, power between and among organizations, organizational units, and individuals will also shift. As I see it, some of us will have the power to dominate, to win, in these circumstances; all of us will have the opportunity to use that power to partner.

I do not mean "to partner" as described in Chapter Three, but rather in the sense of partnership that implies relationship, in which each party has equal status and a certain independence as well as implicit and formal obligations. These are relationships based on trust in all its components—shared vision, respect for competencies, and a full understanding of one another's worldview.

The human race has struggled with the inclination to partner or to dominate for a very long time. Riane Eisler in *The Chalice and the Blade* (1995) reminds us of one of the first recorded merger discussions—a passage in the writings of Thucydides, who chronicled the Peloponnesian War of 431 to 403 B.C.E. "In Thucydides' account of a dialogue between the Athenian emissaries and the representatives of Melos, a small city-state in the Cyclades the Athenians wanted to annex, the Athenians bluntly tell the Melians they are not interested in right or wrong; their interest is only in what is expedient. For 'the question of justice arises only between parties equal in strength while the strong do what they can and the weak suffer what they must'" (p. 118).

Not long ago, I chatted with the director of human resources of a large bank facing the need to "get big or be taken over." She described her organization as a "vacuum cleaner," picking up one smaller bank after another, downsizing each, stripping some of them of their assets, closing others. Survival for this larger bank is everything. The people who work in their organization or who are affected by the merger rush are not "even on the radar screen" of management consideration. Following acquisition, a team moves into the acquired company with a sense of victory, proudly displaying their arrogance, their superiority, and their condescension. They win, always, or at least they have until now.

I believe that most nonprofits will have the opportunity to enter into serious and significant alliances with other organizations in the next five to ten years. Many organizations will not have a choice about this; others will. However free or forced that choice may be, all of us will have choices about how we do this.

We must take care about what we do in the name of survival. The magnitude of change the sector faces may well force us to consider what organizational survival is. At its most basic level, an organization is a package of competencies organized as a repertoire of routines designed to produce a specific outcome. As we discovered in our discussion of culture, it is also in some ways a partnership between employer and employees, a mutually invented reality.

As the environment's turbulence increases, organizational leaders must define for themselves what survival will mean. From both a theoretical and practical perspective, an organization survives if its routines survive, for if the routines survive, the outcome may still be achieved. This perspective should create the recognition that dramatic changes in the administrative superstructure can occur with little effect on the achievement of the outcome. A colleague in health care recently shared his belief that the merger of his small nonprofit into a much larger entity is a "complete success, because nothing at all has changed for our line staff or our consumers."

There are two additional perspectives I would like to share. The first is a view of partnership from the work of Peter Block, in *Stewardship: Choosing Service Over Self-Interest* (1996).

> Partnership carries the intention to balance power between ourselves and those around us. It brings into question the utility of

maintaining consistency and control as cornerstones of management. It comes from the choice to place control close to where the
work is done and not hold it as a prerogative of the middle and
upper classes. It also flows from the choice to yield on consistency
in how we manage, and thus to support local units in creating policies and practices that fit local situations [p. 8].

And the second is from Margaret Wheatley's *Leadership and the
New Science* (1994). As she reminds us:

Innovation is fostered by information gathered from new connections; from insights gained by journeys into other disciplines or
places; from active, collegial networks and fluid, open boundaries.
Innovation arises from ongoing circles of exchange, where information is not just accumulated or stored, but created. Knowledge is
generated anew from connections that weren't there before. When
this information self-organizes, innovations occur, the progeny of
information-rich, ambiguous environments [p. 113].

Perhaps through the nonprofit sector's strongly held values, a
commitment to partnership, and an openness to innovation, we
can invent better, kinder ways to consolidate our organizations
than the private sector has found so far.

In a recent discussion with a colleague at the Boston Foundation who has also written on the subject of restructuring options,
we talked about how much we don't know yet, about how early it
is in this new stage of evolution of the nonprofit sector in which
consolidation is likely to be a dominant strategy. We talked about
the need for continuing study and our hope that best practices for
managing the consolidated entities will soon emerge.

It is perfectly clear to me that the last word has not been written on this subject. It is my hope that the material included here
is a jumping-off place for nonprofit leadership and for colleagues
who research and write for the sector. The future rests with you,
the individuals who lead nonprofits, for it is the sum of your
choices that will determine, not necessarily whether, but how the
sector restructures.

| The MacMillan Matrix

The MacMillan Matrix is a valuable tool that was designed to help nonprofits assess their programs in light of scarce resources. It is used extensively throughout The Support Centers of America Network. Here, with some slight alteration, we use the tool to assist Boards in assessing their overall competitive position in light of future trends and to surface opportunities for working with other organizations. The matrix (see Figure A.1), used in this format, will help answer these critical questions:

- How well does our program portfolio fit with our vision and mission?
- What is the relative competitive strength of each of our programs?
- Do we have programs capable of growth in the environment as we envision it?
- Are we engaged in any services which, if eliminated, would cause consumers irreplaceable loss?
- Should we work cooperatively with another organization to sustain a service or pursue a new opportunity?

Completing the Matrix

To use the matrix, first list all of the programs currently run by the organization as well as any new potential opportunities that have been identified. Assess each program listed according to the four sets of criteria described in this section, bearing in mind the lists of trends and needed competencies developed as part of your strategic planning

---

Note: The MacMillian Matrix is reprinted by permission of JAI Press.

Figure A.1. The MacMillan Matrix.

	High Program Attractiveness (Easy to attract resources for support)		**Low Program Attractiveness** (Difficult to attract resources for support)		
	Alternate Coverage **HIGH**	Alternate Coverage **LOW**	Alternate Coverage **HIGH**	Alternate Coverage **LOW**	
Strong Competitive Position	**1.** Aggressive Competition	**2.** Aggressive Growth	**5.** Reinforce Best Competitor or Find Partner	**6.** "Soul of the Agency"	GOOD FIT
Weak Competitive Position	**3.** Aggressive Divestment	**4.** Invest, Find Partner, or Divest	**7.** Find Partner or Divest	**8.** Find Partner, or Divest	
	9. Aggressive Divestment		**10.** Orderly Divestment		POOR FIT

process (see Chapter One). Make your judgments based on your beliefs about the future. Then place each program in its appropriate cell in the matrix. Assess each program against all the criteria before choosing its appropriate place in the matrix unless otherwise indicated.

Fit

Fit is the degree to which a program belongs or fits within an organization, according to these criteria:

- Congruence with the mission and vision of the organization
- Degree to which the organization can support the program with existing skills and competencies
- Ability to share resources and coordinate activities with other organizational programs

If a program is a good fit, it will be placed somewhere in cells 1 through 8. If a poor fit, it will be placed in cells 9 or 10. (As noted, suspend judgment regarding the specific placement until you see what the other three criteria indicate.)

Program Attractiveness

Program attractiveness is the degree to which a program is attractive to the organization from an economic perspective, as an investment of current and future resources (that is, whether the program easily attracts resources). A program is highly attractive if it is affirmatively ranked on *each* of these criteria:

- Current stable funding
- High appeal to groups providing future support whether consumer fees, grant funds, or both
- Market demand from a large consumer base that is not expected to shrink
- Measurable, reportable program outcomes

If a program is a good fit and is highly attractive, it will be placed in one of the cells labeled 1 through 4. If a poor fit and attractive, it can be placed in cell 9 now; no need for further analysis. If a program is a good fit but is not attractive, it will be placed in one of the cells labeled 5 through 8. If a poor fit and not attractive, it can be placed in cell 10 now.

Alternative Coverage

Alternative coverage is a measure of the existing alternatives for consumers. If there are very few or no comparable providers in the area, coverage is said to be low. If consumers have many other choices to meet their needs, coverage is said to be high.

If the number of competitors is expected to increase significantly in the next three years, label the program as "high coverage."

Programs with good fit, high attractiveness, and high coverage will be placed in either cell 1 or 3; low coverage will put the same programs in cell 2 or 4. Programs with good fit, low attractiveness, and low coverage will be placed in either cell 6 or 8. Programs with good fit, low attractiveness, and high coverage will placed in either cell 5 or 7.

Competitive Position

Competitive position is the degree to which the organization has a stronger capability and potential to deliver these services than current or emerging competitors. "Stronger capability and potential" results from a number of strengths, not just one. Criteria for a competitive position will include a substantial majority of the following:

- Good location and logistical delivery system
- Large reservoir of consumer loyalty and the assurance that consumer choice will continue to govern consumer decisions in the future
- Dominant and growing market share of the target consumers currently served
- Superior quality coupled with the ability to account for quality
- Stable staffing
- A refined understanding of what competencies will be required to provide these services in the future and identified sources and resources to acquire them

- Superior ability to communicate with consumers and other stakeholders
- Cost-effective services and the ability to demonstrate this
- A solid track record for securing grants, contracts, and donations to support this programming

After applying these criteria, you should have found a place for each program in the matrix. Competitive programs with good fit, high attractiveness, and high coverage will be in cell 1; uncompetitive ones in cell 3. Competitive programs with good fit, high attractiveness, and low coverage will be in cell 2; uncompetitive ones in cell 4. Competitive programs with good fit, low attractiveness, and low coverage will be in cell 6; uncompetitive ones in cell 8. Competitive programs with good fit, low attractiveness, and high coverage will in cell 5, and uncompetitive ones in cell 7. The programs with poor fit will be in cell 9 or cell 10, depending on whether or not funds are easily available for them.

Identifying Strengths and Weaknesses in the Program Portfolio

Once you have placed all your current and planned programming on the MacMillan Matrix, you can begin making use of the information. Placement in the various cells indicates organizational choices for strategy relative to this specific programming.

Strategy Cells Explained

Assess your program strengths and weaknesses using the outline given in this section.

- Cell 1. *Aggressive Competition.* There is a major opportunity here, but the organization will have to fight for its share of the market and must expect to invest heavily in marketing efforts to maintain market share. You can make a go of programs in this cell, but placement here indicates that you expect or already have to deal with significant competition for consumers or for contracts and grants to support this programming.

- Cell 2. *Aggressive Growth.* There are substantial resources, plentiful consumers, and few competitors for programs listed here. This programming automatically becomes a high priority for attention as the organization has a significant opportunity to build market share. As others recognize the organization's success, competition will increase—so *timely* investment in growth is imperative.

- Cell 3. *Aggressive Divestment.* This is programming that lacks key aspects of being competitive and also faces stiff competition. It fails to fit with the organization's mission, or the organization lacks the competence to make it competitive—or both. As a result, this programming is a poor prospect for growth and is not likely to survive without extraordinary effort. Plan to close down these programs as soon as possible to conserve resources for more productive activities.

- Cell 4. *Invest, Find Partner, or Divest.* This programming is a worthwhile investment when the organization has resources available for improving its competitive position—after programs in the first two cells have been taken care of. If investment resources do not exist, these programs then become candidates for finding a partner. There is opportunity here due to the availability of resources and low competition that could be pursued with a strategic partner. If neither alternative works out, abandon the programming—it is unlikely to assume a competitive position on its own.

- Cell 5. *Reinforce Best Competitor or Find Partner.* Programs in this cell are competitive but difficult to fund, and stiff competition offers significant alternatives for consumers. Your organization may want to strengthen the competitor that seems to be offering consumers the highest-quality services by transferring the programming to that organization (a difficult decision), or may decide to seek a partner, building volume, consolidating overhead, and reducing cost.

- Cell 6. *"Soul of the Agency."* Programs in Cell 6 are those that the organization is committed to delivering even at the cost of subsidizing them with resources from other programs—and that do not have easy access to resources on their own. Such programming makes a special or unique contribution to the welfare of the organization's consumers and therefore to mission accomplishment, and its elimination may cause consumers irreplaceable loss of services. No organization can afford to support an unlimited number of "soul" programs. Decide which ones you can really carry and make sure your organization maintains a mix of programs able to sustain its operations, or your consumers may lose all your services permanently.

- Cell 7. *Find Partner or Divest.* Partnership may be possible for programs in Cell 7, though a program that winds up in this cell will clearly need investment to be successful. It may be difficult to find another organization willing to partner with a much weaker program, but your organization may be able to offer enticements in the form of capital savings to be derived from adopting an already established program, physical plant, staff, or license for the activity. Without a partner, this programming is both unattractive and noncompetitive and your organization should close it down gradually to ease the strain on consumers that currently make use of it.

- Cell 8. *Find Partner or Divest.* Programs in Cell 8 are also both unattractive and noncompetitive. Here, however, there is little competition. You may be able to partner with a provider of these services that is in a stronger competitive position in a contiguous geographic area, as it is possible that such an organization may want to acquire additional capacity. Raising volume and consolidating overhead may reduce expenses and may make this programming more financially viable. If no such potential partner exists, this programming should be gradually eliminated.

- Cell 9. *Aggressive Divestment.* This programming is a poor fit with the organization's mission and vision or competencies. Unless the organization is willing to change its mission and vision or acquire needed competencies, there is no justification for continuing to invest resources here—even when such resources are readily available.

- Cell 10. *Orderly Divestment.* This programming is both unattractive and a poor fit. However, it is desirable to eliminate these services gradually and if at all possible without harm to consumers.

Outline for a Request for Proposals:

Partner Search

I. Statement of Your Organization's Goal in Issuing the RFP
II. Objectives of the RFP Process
III. Narrative Overview of the Issuing Organization
   A. Brief history
   B. Brief listing of programming
   C. Description of the Board of Directors
   D. Description of current staffing pattern
   E. Description of physical plant
IV. Schedule for the RFP Process
   A. Date of issuance
   B. Deadline for receipt of responses
   C. Period of initial review of responses
   D. Period when interviews will be scheduled
   E. Period for exchange of information as of initial discussions
   F. Evaluation of finalists
   G. Announcement of finalist
   H. Planned date for signing letter of intent
V. Content of Proposals
   A. Description of respondent's organization
      1. State and year of incorporation
      2. Composition of governing body
      3. Names of senior management
      4. Names and locations of principal businesses and programs

     5. Copies of last three annual reports or audited financial statements

  B. Name of individual serving as principal contact in the RFP process

  C. Outcome of the affiliation process as viewed by the respondent

  D. Proposed integration of programming

  E. Description of any contingencies that might interfere with going forward

VI. (Optional) List of Priorities of the Board in Reviewing Responses

Worksheet for Constructing a Response Policy

1. All inquiries concerning our organization's interest in becoming involved in a new venture will be referred to:

   _____

2. The initiative will be tested for early feasibility by:

   _____

3. Yes No The party named in (2) will have the ability to screen out the initiative.

   Yes No The party named in (2) may screen out the initiative with the agreement of:

   _____

4. The party named in (2) may expend up to $_____ to test the feasibility of an initiative. Resources beyond this amount can be expended with the agreement of:

   _____

5. If the initiative is feasible, it will be discussed with the Board president. The Board president will assign it to the _____ Committee for further review.

6. In case a quick response is needed,

   _____

   is empowered to give approval to the party named in (2) to
   pursue the opportunity.

7. In all other cases, the _____
   Committee may screen out an opportunity or recommend it
   to the Board of Directors for pursuit.

8. _____
   will determine the negotiating team for each initiative that is
   approved for pursuit.

| **Sample Letter of Intent**

Letter of Intent

Coalition for Children's Healthy Development

Section 1

This letter of intent is entered into as of April 15, 1998 by and among Child Welfare, Inc., Children's Services, Inc., Lincoln Psychiatric Hospital, The Portal: Community Behavioral Health Services, Inc., The Tripwell School, St. Florian's Home for Children, Inc., collectively known as the Coalition for Children's Healthy Development.

Section 2

The members of the Coalition for Children's Healthy Development have been meeting to explore ways in which they might come together to create a network for the provision of child welfare services for children and families in the region. At this time, they wish to bind the participants to a specific process so as to forge a collective strategy for such a network and to define their mutual obligations within this process.

Section 3. Purposes

The purposes of this letter of intent are

1. *To define the vision, mission, and guiding principles of the new network.*

2. *To define the planning process by which the new network will be designed and established.*
3. *To determine target dates for completion of various aspects of the process.*
4. *To govern the conduct of the parties during the planning period.*

Section 4. Expiration

This Letter of Intent will expire on December 31, 1998. It may be extended by a unanimous vote of the parties.

Section 5. Agreements Reached to Date

The following agreements have been reached to date:

1.   Oretha Johnson, CEO, Children's Services, Inc. will serve as acting chairman of the Coalition for Children's Healthy Development.

2.   The expenses incurred during the process of negotiation will be shared equally among the parties. With the exceptions of The Tripwell School and St. Florian's Home for Children, Inc., each party agrees to forward $5,000 to Child Welfare, Inc., by May 1, 1998. The Tripwell School and St. Florian's agree to forward $4,000 by April 1, 1998, having been credited with expenses they have already assumed on behalf of the Coalition prior to the drafting of this agreement. These funds will be held in a separate checking account, with Child Welfare, Inc., acting as fiscal agent. Anthony Morgan, the CEO of Child Welfare, Inc., and James P. McMahon, President and CEO of The Portal: Community Behavioral Health Services, Inc., will serve as signers for the checking account. Two signatures will not be required to withdraw funds.

3.   Should any party withdraw from the agreement, or should the parties dissolve the agreement, it is agreed that each party will be responsible for an equal share of expenses encumbered to that point in time. Any unencumbered balance remaining from the initial individual deposit will be returned to the withdrawing party or parties.

4.   The parties agree that the following information from their respective organizations will be deposited immediately and will be available to all other members:

a. Most recently completed audited financial statement.
b. A financial statement reflecting revenue and expense through January 1, 1998.
c. A list of current Board members.
d. A list of any and all pending legal actions.
e. Any adverse letters, correspondence, inquiries, reports, subpoenas, or surveys that seriously threaten licensure from the Department of Children and Youth, and any other documents from any Medicaid fraud unit, State Attorney General's Office, or any other governmental entity (or private entity acting on behalf of a governmental agency) received within the last twenty-four months.
f. Any state or federal audit or investigation report relevant to any of the child welfare operations of the organization received within the last twenty-four months.
g. Copies of all licenses and accreditations relating to child welfare operations of the organization.

5.   The services of Michael Grayco, MBA, Management Consultant, have been retained with the clear understanding that no conflict of interest or impropriety exists because of his prior working relationship with Emile Doucet, Executive Director, The Tripwell School.

6.   Based upon their previous discussions, the parties agree that the probable outcome of their deliberations will be (1) a managed care organization (either created or acquired) that is jointly owned by the parties, (2) a comprehensive provider network served by the MCO, and (3) a management services organization that would be supported by sales of administrative services to other organizations. The process described within this letter of intent is designed to yield this outcome. The parties have agreed that the following statements reflect their current mutually determined vision, mission and guiding principles for this planned entity:

Vision

We envision a comprehensive service network designed to meet the needs of children and families in our region. The network will provide a complete array of high-quality services capable of assisting children and families in the least restrictive setting.

Mission

Our mission is to consolidate the efforts of a number of diverse organizations currently providing services to children into a single entity that is capable of providing coordinated, comprehensive, and community-based care that is child and family centered.

Guiding Principles

Child welfare services are defined as including, but not limited to, behavioral health, social services, education, juvenile justice and protective services.

Children who have child welfare needs should have those needs met as close to their home of origin as possible.

Services should be driven by responsiveness to the needs of each child and family.

The network should employ staff who are both bilingual and bicultural, to ensure that services are culturally diverse and culturally competent.

Consistent standards of care will be maintained throughout the network and services will be outcome driven.

The network is committed to continuous quality improvement.

The primary market for the planned entity will be [name of agency], though the network will also seek additional managed care contracts with private insurers if feasible.

The planned entity will provide single source contracting, quality assurance, utilization review, joint training, and MIS support to the network members.

7.   Each party agrees to devote the necessary resources to complete the planning process according to the timeline.

8.   The timeline and the major benchmarks are as follows:

May 14, 1998   Partner assessment completed: consultant's report on review of baseline documents

June 4, 1998   Assessment of existing MCOs completed: consultant's report based on contacts with five organizations identified by the parties.

July 1, 1998   Build-or-acquire decision reached: the parties will determine whether to pursue a strategic partner or to establish their own MCO.

August 15, 1998   Agreement on a plan to proceed:
                     completion of the task list related to the
                     build-or-acquire decision.
September 30, 1998 Approval by all Boards of plan to proceed.

9.   It is agreed that the following will govern closure on the final agreement: The Board of Directors of each organization shall consider the recommendations and shall either accept or reject their participation. If the plan is agreed to by the Boards of Directors, then the parties shall enter into definitive agreements to carry out the terms and conditions of the plan. If one or more parties to this agreement choose not to participate in the planned entity, it is understood that the remaining parties have the right to pursue the creation of the entity, choosing other additional partners as they see fit.

Section 6. Conditions of Conduct

The parties have agreed to the following conditions of conduct during the period covered by the letter of intent. Failure to comply with these conditions of conduct will give the other parties just cause to suspend, modify, or dissolve the agreement with a member or members.

1.   *Partner assessment.* The parties have agreed to deposit the list of documents as outlined above at Child Welfare, Inc. These documents are available for representatives of the parties to review. A list of individuals from each party who will have access to the documents will be forwarded to the Acting Chairman. In addition, the parties have secured the services of Michael Grayco to review the documents. He will raise any pertinent questions or concerns with the parties and will prepare a report to all of the parties by June 4, 1998.

2.   *Discussions with other organizations.* Given the state of environmental change, it is expected that the several parties will be approached by other entities attempting to accomplish similar aims: that is, who are seeking (1) a managed care organization (either created or acquired) that is jointly owned by the parties, (2) a comprehensive provider network of child welfare services served by the MCO, and (3) a management services organization

that would be supported by sales of administrative services to other organizations. The parties agree to inform one another of all of these contacts and discussions.

3. *Noncompetition.* The parties agree that no party to this agreement will serve as an incorporator of a venture that competes with the potential venture outlined within this letter of intent. This agreement will bind the parties during the period covered by the letter of intent. This agreement will also cover any party that withdraws from this agreement prior to the expiration of the letter of intent. If a question arises as to whether a particular set of discussions is, in fact, competitive with this effort, each of the parties agree that the situation will be discussed in a joint meeting of the parties. If the majority of the parties object to the continued discussions, the party in question will agree to end the discussions forthwith. This provision will not bind the parties if the Coalition dissolves.

4. *Internal and public announcements.*

a. No public statements to the press will be made by any party without the approval of the others.

b. In describing this letter of intent to employees of the members, it is agreed that it will be described as follows: "This letter of intent constitutes an exploration of a possible network."

c. It is agreed the highest-ranking representative to the negotiations will be the official spokespersons for each party. It is also agreed that Boards, officers, and employees will refer all press inquiries to the official spokespersons.

5. *Confidentiality.* It is well recognized that during the negotiation process and during the process of partner assessment, the parties will undoubtedly exchange information that may be sensitive or proprietary. The parties therefore agree to the following rules of conduct relative to the confidentiality of the materials exchanged.

a. Each party recognizes that failure to adhere to the confidentiality agreements may result in damage to the others.

b. None of the exchanged materials will be used to the detriment of any party and all who have access to the materials will be instructed as to their confidential nature.

c. Each party agrees to inform the others if the exchanged materials are subpoenaed or if asked to give a deposition as to their contents.
d. All materials will be returned to their owners and no copies will be kept, even if an agreement is not reached.
e. The parties agree to exempt one another from liability for any inadvertent inaccuracies in the exchanged materials.
f. Information that becomes generally available to the public by another means is exempted from these provisions.
g. Any party shall be entitled to injunctive relief, without having to prove the inadequacy of other remedies at law and without being required to post bond or other security, against any other party who fails to adhere to the confidentiality agreements contained herein.

Section 7. Responsibility

On behalf of the parties, the following individuals will carry out the responsibilities outlined in the letter of intent.

Lincoln Psychiatric Hospital: Paul Logan, Vice President, Chief Operating Officer

Child Welfare, Inc., Inc.: Anthony Morgan, Executive Director

The Tripwell School: Emile Doucet, Executive Director

The Portal: Community Behavioral Health Services, Inc., Inc.: James P. McMahon, President/CEO

Children's Services, Inc.: Oretha Johnson, M.S., President/CEO

St. Florian's Home for Children, Inc.: Glenda Diamonte, Executive Director

Section 8. Survival

Section 6.5 concerning confidentiality will survive this letter of intent in perpetuity.

Section 9. Counterparts

This letter of intent may be executed in multiple counterparts each of which will be seen as an original.

Section 10. Governing Law

This letter of intent will be governed and construed by the laws of the State of [Name].

Section 11. Signatures and Dates

Lincoln Psychiatric Hospital

_____   _____
Paul Logan, Vice President, Chief   Date
Operating Officer

Child Welfare, Inc.

_____   _____
Anthony Morgan, Executive Director   Date

The Tripwell School

_____   _____
Emile Doucet, Executive Director   Date

The Portal: Community Behavioral Health Services, Inc.

_____   _____
James P. McMahon, President/CEO   Date

Children's Services, Inc.

_____   _____
Oretha Johnson, M.S., President/CEO   Date

| **Focus Group Questions**

The culture of an organization is encoded in the images, metaphors, artifacts, beliefs, values, norms, rituals, language, stories, legends, myths, and other symbolic constructs that give form to the experience of everyday organizational life.

The following questions can be used as source material for focus group interviews.

1. What are the principal images or metaphors that people use to describe the organization? *Examples: "This organization is like a many-headed monster." "This organization is like a very fragile antique vase."*
2. What physical impression does the organization and its furnishings create? Does this vary from one place to another? *Examples: "Modern, cool, businesslike." "Messy and disorganized."*
3. How are visitors greeted or welcomed?
4. What are the formal processes for welcoming and providing orientation for new employees? What are the informal processes?
5. What beliefs and values dominate the organization officially? Unofficially?
6. What are the main dos and don'ts? *Examples: "Always come to work at least ten minutes early." "Don't ever be late for meetings with [some individual or group]."*
7. What are the main ceremonies and rituals and what purposes do they serve?

Note: These questions have been adapted from *Creative Organization Theory: A Resource Book* (Morgan, 1989). Reprinted by permission of Sage Publications, Inc.

8. What language dominates everyday discourse? If professional jargon is used, what kind of jargon is it? What clichés or buzzwords can you identify?

9. What are the primary stories or legends about the organization's history that people tell? Choose one story that strikes you as particularly important and share it with the group.

10. What actions are formally rewarded? What actions are informally rewarded? What actions are formally punished? What actions are informally punished?

11. If we were to eavesdrop on a typical group of employees engaged in informal conversation, what topics might we hear about?

12. Name the three most influential people in the organization. For each, what characteristics do you feel relate to their influence?

13. Are there identifiable subcultures (groups that seem to do their own thing)? What makes them different? Are they in harmony with the mainstream culture or in conflict?

14. If there are subcultures, what functions do these groups serve for their members? Is the overall effect on the organization positive or negative?

15. If you had an issue that needed to be communicated to your immediate superior, what form of communication would you use?

Recommended Readings

Allison, M., and Kaye, J. *Strategic Planning for Nonprofit Organizations: A Practical Guide and Workbook.* New York: Wiley, 1997.

Astrachan, J. *Mergers, Acquisitions, and Employee Anxiety.* New York: Praeger, 1990.

Badaracco, J. L., Jr. *The Knowledge Link: How Firms Compete Through Strategic Alliances.* Boston: Harvard Business School, 1991.

Bergquist, W., Betwee, J., and Meuel, D. *Building Strategic Relationships: How to Extend Your Organization's Reach Through Partnerships, Alliances, and Joint Ventures.* San Francisco: Jossey-Bass, 1995.

Block, P. *Stewardship: Choosing Service Over Self-Interest.* San Francisco: Berrett-Koehler, 1996.

Blumberg, A., and Wiener, W. "One From Two: Facilitating an Organizational Merger." *Journal of Applied Behavioral Science,* 1971, 7(1), 87–102.

Buono, A. F., and Bowditch, J. L. *The Human Side of Mergers and Acquisitions: Managing Collisions Between People, Cultures, and Organizations.* San Francisco: Jossey-Bass, 1989.

Buono, A. F., Bowditch, J. L., and Lewis, J. W. "When Cultures Collide: The Anatomy of a Merger." *Human Relations,* 1983, 38(5), 447–500.

Cartwright, S., and Cooper, C. L. *Mergers and Acquisitions: The Human Side.* Oxford, England: Butterworth-Heinemann, 1992a.

Cartwright, S., and Cooper, C. L. "The Psychological Impact of Merger and Acquisition on the Individual: A Study of Building Society Managers." *Human Relations,* 1992b, 46(3), 327–347.

Cartwright, S., and Cooper, C. L. *Managing Mergers, Acquisitions, and Strategic Alliances: Integrating People and Cultures.* Oxford, England: Butterworth-Heinemann, 1996.

Daly, J. P. "The Effects of Anger on Negotiations over Mergers and Acquisitions." *Negotiation Journal,* Jan. 1991, pp. 31–39.

Eisler, R. *The Chalice and the Blade: Our History, Our Future.* San Francisco: HarperCollins, 1995.

Fish, A. B. "How to Make a Merger Work." *Fortune,* Jan. 1994, pp. 66–69.

Greenleaf, R. K. *The Servant As Leader.* Indianapolis: Robert K. Greenleaf Center, 1991.

Hampden-Turner, C. *Creating Corporate Culture.* Reading, Mass.: Addison Wesley, 1990.

Hopkins, B. R. *The Law of Tax-Exempt Organizations.* (6th ed.). New York: Wiley, 1992.

Kanter, R. "Collaborative Advantage: The Art of Alliances." *Harvard Business Review,* July/Aug. 1994, pp. 96–108.

Kodama, "Technology Fusion," *Harvard Business Review,* July–August 1992.

Kohler, A. *The Organizational Dynamics of Mergers and Acquisitions.* Unpublished paper, Sept. 1996.

Lewicki, R. J., and Litterer, J. A. *Negotiation.* Homewood, Ill.: Irwin, 1985.

McCambridge, R., and Weis, M. F. *The Rush to Merge.* Boston: Boston Foundation, 1997.

Morgan, G. *Creative Organization Theory: A Resource Book.* Thousand Oaks, Calif.: Sage, 1989.

National Center for Nonprofit Boards. *Beyond Collaboration: Strategic Restructuring of Nonprofit Organizations.* Washington, D.C.: National Center for Nonprofit Boards, 1997.

Rock, M. L., Rock, S. H., and Sikora, M. (Eds.). *The Mergers and Acquisitions Handbook.* New York: McGraw Hill, 1994.

Rothman, J., Erlich, J. L., and Teresa, J. G. *Changing Organizations and Community Programs.* Thousand Oaks, Calif.: Sage, 1981.

Sanders, M. I. *Partnerships and Joint Ventures Involving Tax-Exempt Organizations.* New York: Wiley, 1994.

Segil, L. *Intelligent Business Alliances.* New York: Random House, 1996.

Smith, P. B., and Peterson, M. F. *Leadership, Organizations, and Culture.* Thousand Oaks, Calif.: Sage, 1989.

Taylor, J., Austin, M. J., and Caputo, R. K. "Managing Mergers of Human Service Agencies: People, Programs, and Procedures." *Child Welfare,* 1992, *71*(1), 37–52.

Ury, W., and Fisher, R. *Getting to Yes.* New York: Penguin, 1991.

Volunteer Trustees Foundation. *When Your Community Hospital Goes Up for Sale.* Washington, D.C.: Volunteer Trustees Foundation, 1996.

Walker, G. A. "Culture Collisions in Mergers and Acquisitions." In P. J. Frost (Ed.), *Organizational Culture.* Thousand Oaks, Calif.: Sage, 1985.

Wheatley, M. J. *Leadership and the New Science: Learning About Organization from an Orderly Universe.* San Francisco: Berrett-Koehler, 1994.

Zweig, P. "The Case Against Mergers." *Business Week,* Oct. 1995, pp. 122–130.

Index

Printed in the United States
34391LVS00002BD/30